THE ORIGINS OF
HAMILTON'S FISCAL POLICIES

by Donald F. Swanson

University of Florida Monographs
SOCIAL SCIENCES
No. 17, Winter 1963

UNIVERSITY OF FLORIDA PRESS / GAINESVILLE, FLORIDA

EDITORIAL COMMITTEE

Social Sciences Monographs

ARTHUR W. THOMPSON, *Chairman*
Professor of History

RALPH H. BLODGETT
Professor of Economics

ARTHUR W. COMBS
Professor of Education

MANNING J. DAUER
Professor of Political Science

T. LYNN SMITH
Professor of Sociology

WILSE B. WEBB
Professor of Psychology

―――――――――――――――――――――――――――――――――――――

LIBRARY OF CONGRESS
CATALOGUE CARD NO. 63-63264

PRINTED BY DOUGLAS PRINTING CO.
JACKSONVILLE, FLORIDA

CONTENTS

ACKNOWLEDGMENTS

The writer wishes to express his deepest appreciation to two of his former professors, Dr. Manning J. Dauer and Dr. John N. Webb, both of the University of Florida, for their generous giving of time and suggestions at various stages of preparing this study. It was Professor Dauer who first interested me in the study of Hamilton and the Federalist Era. I am especially indebted to Professor Webb for his amazing ability to ask those questions which move an argument to a more meaningful direction.

Others who have read the manuscript in an earlier form, and to whom I am grateful, include Professors Clement H. Donovan, Edgar S. Dunn, Elmo L. Jackson, and Allen M. Sievers. All remaining deficiencies in the study are, of course, my own responsibility.

A special note of thanks is extended to my wife, Carolyn, who has given me constant encouragement during the writing and preparation of the study.

D. F. S.

1. THE HISTORY OF A CONTROVERSY

A nation must reach a certain degree of maturity and sophistication, ordinarily, before it becomes interested in its birth and origins. Certainly such an interest would not have been expected from men absorbed in the task of exploiting the resources of a new continent. One aspect of nascent American national life — the origins of the fiscal policies of Alexander Hamilton — did not wait upon the scholars of a more sophisticated age for its examination. Twice during the nation's history, concern over the origins of these policies has become rather widespread, first during Hamilton's own lifetime, and again in the late nineteenth century. The Hamiltonian policies that were especially singled out for such treatment are his funding system, sinking fund, and national bank.

Scholarly opinion of the late nineteenth century was almost unanimous in its judgment concerning the origin of Hamilton's fiscal policies: Hamilton was found guilty of importing English principles of finance. The subject had always been presented in a controversial fashion, as a choice between the extreme positions of whether Hamilton's policies were his original inventions or whether they were mere copies of the English models. Since Hamilton had no special training in finance, and since evidence of his copying English fiscal policies was abundant, the historically popular outlook on the question has been that of accepting the position that Hamilton was heavily dependent on English precedents for his fiscal policies. Even a recent writer lends support to this historical judgment by saying: "They [Hamilton's fiscal policies] were not original — they were almost slavishly imitative of the English system."[1]

RATIONALE BEHIND THE ENGLISH IMITATION THESIS

The underlying explanation for the early and continued interest in the origins of Hamilton's fiscal policies appears to be the fact that certain individuals have intended either to discredit Hamilton's political

1. Mildred Buzek Otenasek, "Alexander Hamilton's Fiscal Policies" (unpublished Ph.D. dissertation, Johns Hopkins University, 1939), p. 52.

reputation or to show that Hamilton's policies were based upon erroneous theoretical principles. Chronologically, the first motive was to discredit Hamilton's reputation, which, of course, grew out of the great political battle of the Hamiltonian era — the struggle between the Federalists and the party of Jefferson. The Jeffersonians wanted control of the Federal government, and they no doubt knew the importance of fiscal policy in directing the future economic development of the new nation. Jefferson was admittedly an advocate of a primarily agricultural society. His remarks about the "mobs of great cities" and the necessity of letting "our workshops remain in Europe" are well known. To Jefferson, "the proportion which the aggregate of the other classes of citizens bears in any State to that of its husbandmen, is the proportion of its unsound to its healthy parts, and is a good enough barometer whereby to measure its degree of corruption."[2] In contrast, Hamilton was in favor of what today would be called a balanced economy. He wanted to erect upon the agricultural base of the nation a well-developed network of manufacturing and financial centers. Both Hamilton and Jefferson knew that fiscal policy could be employed to give direction to economic growth, and at the same time to preserve or destroy an elite based upon the dominant economic base of the country. In particular, the elite preserved or destroyed might be the landed aristocracy of Virginia; and the elite created to take its place might be that based upon commercial wealth.

Jefferson's method for combating Hamiltonian policies was not the same as the method he advocated for other types of "error," that is, reason and free inquiry. Instead, he used the contemporary distaste for things English to discredit Hamilton's fiscal policies on the grounds that they were importations of "English principles."[3] Jefferson's charge was not difficult to promulgate, as there were enough striking similarities between Hamilton's fiscal policies and those of the English Chancellors of the Exchequer, especially Pitt, to convince any person who had the slightest suspicion of Hamilton's designs. This mode of attack against Hamilton had been developing for some time with respect to his monarchical political ideas. The picture of Hamilton as an Anglophile would

2. Thomas Jefferson, "Notes on Virginia," *The Life and Selected Writings of Thomas Jefferson*, eds. Adrienne Koch and William Peden (New York: The Modern Library, 1944), p. 280.

3. Jefferson to Richard M. Johnson, March 10, 1808, *The Writings of Thomas Jefferson*, ed. Andrew A. Lipscomb (Washington: The Thomas Jefferson Memorial Association, 1903), XII, 9-10.

be complete if it were generally believed that his fiscal policies also were of English origin.

The Jeffersonian crusade against the Hamiltonian system also involved the moral issue of who should pay off the large national debt incurred during the Revolution. Hamilton was indifferent to the ethics of the question: the conclusion rested on economic considerations. Jefferson, however, was firmly committed to the belief that the "laws of nature" imposed no obligation on a new generation to pay the debts of the old generation.[4] The Jeffersonian position was that it was immoral to bind a succeeding generation by the debts of the present. Based upon his calculation of the length of a generation, Jefferson reached the conclusion that a national debt must be paid within a maximum of nineteen years.

Jefferson's obsession for rapid repayment of the debt made him especially critical of Hamilton's sinking fund. According to the prevailing idea of a sinking fund, such a policy supposedly would pay off a national debt within a relatively short period of time. But Hamilton, according to Jefferson, was using it and other fiscal policies as a "puzzle to exclude popular understanding and inquiry."[5] Jefferson's argument was that Hamilton purposely designed the operation and administration of the sinking fund in a complicated and mystifying manner in order to cover up the fact that the debt was not being reduced. In the process, Hamilton had created a "machine" for the corruption of the legislature. Because Hamilton's sinking fund was not paying off the debt, Jefferson reached the conclusion that Hamilton "wishes it never to be paid."[6] The essence of English fiscal policies, according to Jefferson, was perpetuity financing. The related evils of paper money, stockjobbing, speculation, and a moneyed interest were the outgrowths of the English system.[7] With a conviction of this sort, Jefferson referred to Hamilton as "the servile copyist of Mr. Pitt."[8]

Between the end of the Hamiltonian-Jeffersonian era and 1860, any interest in the origins of Hamilton's fiscal policies had all but disappeared. The main traces of the controversy are to be found in the writings of authors interested in the banking problems of that period,

4. Jefferson to John W. Eppes, June 24, 1813, *ibid.*, XIII, 272.
5. "The Anas," *ibid.*, I, 271.
6. Jefferson to Washington, September 9, 1792, *ibid.*, VIII, 401.
7. Jefferson to General Gates, May 30, 1797, *ibid.*, IX, 391.
8. Jefferson to Monroe, May 26, 1795, *The Works of Thomas Jefferson*, ed. Paul L. Ford (New York: G. P. Putnam's Sons, 1904), VIII, 176.

especially those who were opposed to the Second Bank of the United States. William Cobbett, for example, in his biography of Andrew Jackson, wrote vehemently of a national bank as a "monster of paper money."[9] Cobbett's argument was that Hamilton had patterned the First Bank of the United States as much as possible after the Bank of England. The point of his argument seems to have been that, being English in origin, the national bank was *ipso facto* undemocratic and unfit for American soil.

LENDING INTELLECTUAL RESPECTABILITY TO THE ENGLISH IMITATION THESIS

The observation that the controversy over the origins of Hamilton's fiscal policies grew out of a political struggle and had the intent to discredit Hamilton does not explain the preservation over the years of what can be called the Jeffersonian English imitation thesis. By 1860, Hamilton's three fiscal policies had almost become historical curiosities. The funding system, as will be shown, was merely a means of handling a special problem created by the financing of the Revolution; the Bank of the United States and its twin of 1816 had long since fallen in political defeat; and the sinking fund passed out of existence in 1834, when the national debt was completely extinguished. But with the outbreak of the Civil War and the prospects of a rising national debt, renewed interest arose for the sinking fund scheme of Hamilton. In 1861, Secretary of the Treasury Chase included a sinking fund among his proposed expedients for meeting the financial problems introduced by war.

The sinking fund legislation that followed, however, was not rigidly observed. When peace returned, the law was not regarded as binding by Secretary of the Treasury Hugh McCulloch. Nevertheless, the Civil War experience indicated that Hamiltonian fiscal ideas had not been altogether forgotten.

In the decade beginning in 1880, the nation faced a new and unusual type of emergency, namely, the problem of what to do with the budget surpluses that were chronically plaguing the Federal government. Surpluses, ranging from a low of $63 million to a high of $145 million (the latter figure representing approximately one-half of average total expenditures), appeared in every year of that decade. The advocates of a high protective tariff were not, of course, willing to accept the solu-

9. *Life of Andrew Jackson* (n.p., 1845), p. 176.

tion of decreased government revenues, and the social philosophy of the time would not permit a higher level of government expenditures. Presidents, Congressmen, businessmen, bankers, and all agreed that the surpluses had to be returned to the economy. It has been reported that "one year's surplus revenue retained by the treasury meant a reduction in the monetary circulation of at least one-twelfth."[10] Not much could be done in the way of debt redemption, because by 1886 practically all of the debt subject to redemption within many years to come had been canceled.

One solution to the problem of the surpluses remained, that is, reviving the unenforced sinking fund. Open market purchases of debt not redeemable would return the excess revenues to the economy. President Benjamin Harrison, 1889-1893, justified the revival of the sinking fund as being the only lawful and proper solution.[11] But it eventually became quite apparent that the sinking fund purchases were creating new problems, problems perhaps worse than the one intended to be remedied. One such problem was that the premium on the government bonds was steadily rising. Purchases at high premiums made the operation costly and subject to considerable criticism. It was charged that, in effect, the government was paying bonuses to bondholders, and promoting speculation.

The most serious problem attending the revival of the sinking fund was its impact on the money supply. Between 1880 and 1890, the volume of national bank notes shrank from $344,505,000 to $185,970,000.[12] In purchasing government bonds, the sinking fund was buying up the bonds that were needed to back the national bank note issues. The high premiums on bonds made it unprofitable for banks to keep them. Between 1879 and 1890, the total debt declined from $1,996,000,000 to $891,000,000. During the same period the price level declined continuously, and agitation developed for various reforms, including the free coinage of silver. By the end of his administration, President Harrison changed his mind about the sinking fund as a solution to the problem of the surpluses, and recommended the repeal of the law.

At this juncture in American fiscal policy history, the economists

10. Davis Rich Dewey, *National Problems 1885-1897*, Vol. XXIV: *The American Nation: A History* (New York: Harper & Brothers, 1907), p. 59.

11. Lewis H. Kimmel, *Federal Budget and Fiscal Policy 1789-1958* (Washington: The Brookings Institution, 1959), p. 75.

12. Davis Rich Dewey, *Financial History of the United States* (6th ed.; New York: Longmans, Green and Co., 1918), p. 412.

entered the origins controversy. Their purpose was rather obvious: they wanted the nation to abandon a policy which required the income of a sinking fund to be inviolably used for the purchase of government debt. According to Henry C. Adams, one of the first of the economists to enter the controversy, the sinking fund had created a "danger to the permanency of the banking system":

> It is hardly necessary to speak at length of the nature of the embarrassment under which the banking system lies. The difficulty springs from the fact that the bonds upon which it is most profitable for the banks to do business are the only bonds which the government is at liberty to pay.

Either the banking laws or those pertaining to the sinking fund had to be changed. Adams was in favor of a change in the latter: "The problem . . . might be solved by amending the banking law, but we are only interested in proposals for its solution by some modifications of the policy of debt-payment." And, again, "It will probably be wise for the sinking fund law to be repealed, or, at least, for its operations to be suspended."[13]

The lingering and "pernicious"[14] monster of Hamiltonian finance, the sinking fund, must go. The objective was to show that Hamilton's sinking fund was based on extremely fallacious principles. An exposé of these errors would bring about a reappraisal and change in debt management policies.

The problem remains of explaining why the economists were led to the topic of the origins of Hamilton's fiscal policies. If Hamilton held to erroneous ideas on public finance, then it was only necessary to expose them to view. But by confining their investigations to this side of the Atlantic, that is, to Hamilton's own words, the economists were unable to prove decisively that Hamilton's theoretical foundations were fallacious. It was necessary, therefore, to trace Hamilton's fiscal policies to English fiscal policies in order to bolster their case. It was then a relatively simple matter to point out the preposterous ideas associated with a sinking fund. Adams used this approach in arguing that it was not necessary to show that Hamilton "formally" expressed confidence in the erroneous principles of the sinking fund. By tracing the origins

13. Henry C. Adams, *Public Debts* (New York: D. Appleton and Company, 1887), pp. 274-79.
14. *Ibid.*, p. 282.

of his policies to the English, and by showing the similarities between the two countries' policies, inference and observation would lead to the conclusion that Hamilton's fiscal policies were "wholly English,"[15] and therefore, in their minds, erroneous.

During the time in which Hamilton's reputation was being subjected to harsh treatment by the economists, Charles F. Dunbar published in 1888 an essay on the origins of Hamilton's fiscal policies. Dunbar believed that Hamilton's reputation deserved a fate better than it was receiving in the hands of the economists. His purpose was rather complex: on the basis of his extensive study of the Hamiltonian administration, he wanted to make a definitive treatment of the origins controversy that would clearly show that Hamilton, although guilty of copying English fiscal policies, was, in general, a rather "great financial statesman."[16]

In view of the support given by Dunbar's article to the English imitation thesis, it is not easy to understand Dunbar's admiration of Hamilton. Dunbar attempted to reconcile his position by avoiding the conclusion that Hamilton's theoretical orientation was wholly fallacious, but he based his attempt on a very doubtful point, namely, that English fiscal policies, especially Pitt's, were not fallacious. To clear Hamilton, Dunbar had to clear Pitt. Dunbar was perplexed by the obvious fact that Hamilton's administration was successful. If successful, how could it have been based on error? This was the special message that Dunbar wanted to communicate, while documenting Hamilton's heavy reliance on English precedents.

Four years later, in 1892, Edward Ross wrote an article on sinking funds that would have pleased Jefferson immensely. In examining the origins of Hamilton's sinking fund, Ross found that Pitt's sinking fund was "imitated by Hamilton." But Ross was not impressed by Hamilton's administration as Dunbar had been, and he did not hesitate to emphasize that "our early finance was too much influenced by English precedent."[17]

The changed economic conditions after 1888 were reflected in Ross's article. The problem of the surpluses was diminishing. In 1891, the surplus dropped to the comparatively low level of $37,240,000; in 1892

15. *Ibid.*, pp. 263-65.
16. "Some Precedents Followed by Alexander Hamilton," *Economic Essays,* ed. O. M. W. Sprague (New York: The Macmillan Company, 1904), p. 93.
17. "Sinking Funds," *Publications of the American Economic Association* (American Economic Association, 1892), VII, 54, 98.

it was only $9,914,000.[18] After Dunbar had written, the Republicans had gained power and passed the McKinley Tariff of 1890. "In order to reduce the revenue so as to relieve the troublesome problem of a surplus," Dewey had pointed out, "protection on some commodities was extended to the point of practically excluding foreign importations."[19] The outcome of the tariff reduced Ross's task merely to putting the finishing touches on the brief resurgence of a Hamiltonian policy. Ross's arguments concerning the "dangers" inherent in a "rigid" sinking fund were probably convincing enough to erase any lingering beliefs in the efficacy of such a policy.

STATE OF THE ENGLISH IMITATION THESIS

Present-day opinion on Hamilton's financial system is curiously mixed. Although the political motives for the maintenance of the English imitation thesis no longer exist, it would seem evident from an examination of most works on Hamilton and America's early fiscal history that the ideas emerging from the special pleading of political factions and economists of an earlier era, though tempered by the passage of time, linger on. Consequently Hamilton is sometimes thought of at the same time as a great financial statesman and as a copyist of English fiscal policies. The appraisal is somewhat inconsistent, in view of our knowledge of the fiasco that took place in eighteenth-century English finance. Hamilton is also sometimes pictured as a financial statesman whose administration was subject to praise on the grounds that his policies were essential to the successful establishment of the new nation, and at the same time subject to condemnation on the grounds that his policies constituted means that were the antithesis of the ideals of the Revolution. In short, Hamilton's policies were necessary evils. This "Machiavellian" image of Hamilton is equally inconsistent with the English imitation thesis, because it implies that Hamilton's financial policies were sound. The Jeffersonian argument assumed otherwise.

Other arguments can be advanced to place the Jeffersonian English imitation thesis in doubt. The very fact that the economists felt it necessary to trace the origins of the fiscal policies in order to prove them erroneous makes one wonder whether, in fact, Hamilton's policies were thoroughly English. If Hamilton's fiscal policies were not based on false English principles, then it is quite likely that his fiscal policies might

18. Dewey, *Financial History of the U. S.*, p. 448.
19. Dewey, *National Problems*, p. 175.

have differed in operation from the English policies. Equally important is the consideration that the objective or purpose of fiscal policy might have been significantly different in America. The theory of the sinking fund in England led to exaggerated hopes about the liquidation of the English national debt. If Hamilton did not share the theory, then he might have had other objectives or purposes in establishing a sinking fund.

The many similarities between Hamilton's fiscal policies and the English models would make altogether untenable any attempt to divorce Hamilton's policies from those of the English. This would be true also of attempts to deny the dependence upon the English heritage of many American institutions. But little is heard of these other institutions' being blind imitations. In practically every other phase of American development, historians, political scientists, and economists grant that the New World environment produced important modifications in the transplanted Old World institutions. Parrington, for example, acknowledges that American political thought — though traceable to English political thought — came to conclusions that differentiated it broadly from the English original.[20] By the end of the eighteenth century, a sufficiently distinctive intellectual life and social environment had emerged to make the new nation much more than a mere replica of the Old World.

It would seem highly improbable that, in the development of the new nation, the changed conditions would produce significant changes in Old World institutions in other spheres and not in fiscal policy. The changed intellectual life and national problems would be expected to have their impact on fiscal policy as well as on politics and religion. Thus, when contrasted with the known pattern of modification and development of other transplanted institutions, the English imitation thesis of the origins of Hamilton's fiscal policies would seem to be inconsistent and of dubious validity.

REPLACING THE ENGLISH IMITATION THESIS

Considering what has been previously stated, it would seem that any new interpretation of Alexander Hamilton's fiscal policies must meet certain rather obvious specifications. The first is based upon the indisputable fact that several close and striking parallels do exist between Hamilton's fiscal policies and those of the English. These parallels,

20. Vernon Louis Parrington, *Main Currents in American Thought* (New York: Harcourt, Brace and Company, 1927), I, 292.

therefore, must be reconciled in any interpretation of Hamilton's fiscal policies that departs from the Jeffersonian view. In the chapters that follow, the similarities between the Hamiltonian and English systems will become apparent. These parallels, which constitute the proofs of the nineteenth-century economists, are summarized in Chapter 7.

A new interpretation also would have to support the view, already expressed, that any analysis designed to discredit Hamilton's fiscal policies almost invariably takes the form of tracing their origins to England. Lastly, it would be expected that a new interpretation could reconcile, on the one hand, the image of Hamilton as a great, though somewhat "Machiavellian," statesman who providentially appeared on the American scene at the beginning of its national life — in the manner of Rousseau's "lawgiver" — and who wisely laid the needed foundation of a sound economy; and, on the other hand, the conflicting image of Hamilton as a copyist of erroneous English fiscal policies.

The procedure that will be followed in Chapters 2 through 6 can be briefly summarized. Chapters 2 and 3 examine the supposed models for Hamiltonian finance, the English fiscal policies. Attention will be directed both to the superficial appearances of these English fiscal policies, their forms and apparatus; and to more fundamental matters, including developments that led to their establishment, the purposes for which they were designed, their operation, and their theoretical foundations.

Chapter 4 lays the groundwork for the major task of studying the contrasting motives, purposes, and theoretical foundations of Hamilton's fiscal policies. With that end in view, the American financial and debt problems and policies prior to 1789 are analyzed. This chapter relies heavily upon the writings of Alexander Hamilton, Robert Morris, and others, the various sources of popular opinion concerning financial questions, and also the preconstitutional government documents.

The remainder of this study draws almost completely upon the letters and state papers of Hamilton, the writings of Hamilton's associates and political foes, and also legislative debates, statutes, and other original sources. Chapters 5 and 6 concentrate attention on the establishment and operation of Hamilton's fiscal policies. It is in Chapter 6 that a new interpretation of Hamilton's fiscal policies will begin to unfold. Chapter 7, the final chapter, will combine the emerging pattern with the groundwork laid in the previous chapters, in order to arrive at the conclusions of this study.

2. ENGLISH FISCAL POLICIES: THE FUNDING SYSTEM AND THE BANK OF ENGLAND

The radical schemes of projectors of one era frequently survive to become the orthodoxy of a subsequent age. The fiscal policies that flourished in England at the time Alexander Hamilton took office, and which were then regarded with such high esteem, had a very unorthodox beginning. They were products or, rather, schemes of men who lived near the beginning of the era of nation-building. Public finance was in its infancy. It was no longer the problem of a king who had been embarrassed by his prodigality, but of statesmen who were solidifying national power and expanding the nation's influence and domain. To an important extent, these statesmen relied on precedents both crude in quality and few in number. These men had to be creative during a period in which public finance was in a primitive stage. The study of the rise of public finance during this era is interesting in itself, but it is especially instructive from the viewpoint of the controversy over the origins of Hamilton's fiscal policies, because it can show clearly the nature and purpose of the English fiscal policies. An examination of the Bank of England and the English funding system in this chapter, and of the English sinking fund in the next chapter, will provide a useful framework to contrast the nature and purposes of Alexander Hamilton's fiscal policies.

ORIGIN OF THE FUNDING SYSTEM AND THE BANK OF ENGLAND

From 1688 to 1795, a span of 107 years, England had forty-seven years of war and only sixty years of peace. One of England's central fiscal problems, therefore, was raising the necessary funds to conduct war. The Glorious Revolution, which marked the beginning of the period under examination, meant, for one thing, that England had inherited a war. William III was dedicated to the task of defeating Louis XIV, but the conduct of the war against France was complicated by the lack of sufficient revenue.

Financial Difficulties of William III. — At the beginning of the last decade of the seventeenth century, existing sources of revenue in England were yielding less than £2,000,000 annually, and William needed

11

over £5,000,000 to conduct the war and to give financial aid to his allies. The situation was improved only slightly by the levying of new taxes. Taxes were introduced on land rents, windows in houses, births, marriages, burials, bachelors, widowers, peddlers, hackney-coaches in London, and legal documents. Tax rates were increased on the customs and excises, but it was impossible to expect much additional revenue from taxation, because of both the defects in the tax collection system and the political situation after the revolution — William feared burdening his new subjects too heavily with taxes. The prospects of financing the war by borrowing appeared equally dim, since, because of the feared instability of the revolutionary establishment, the public credit was very low. The desperate situation that confronted William might never have been surmounted if the King had not been served by an able financier, Charles Montagu, who was willing to innovate in English finance. Other countries, notably Holland, France, and Italy, had been using expedients that had gone untried in England. From these, Montagu introduced into England a new principle of borrowing, one based on the idea of mortgaging taxes to the public creditors, not for the payment of both interest and principal within a short period of time — the older system of anticipation, but for the payment merely of the interest. The advantage of such a scheme was that, for a given amount of mortgaged taxes, it permitted the raising of a larger loan than was possible under the system of anticipation.

Montagu's problem was to discover the particular type of borrowing technique that would place into practice the new principle of borrowing. He first experimented in this direction in 1692, when he tried to raise £1,000,000 with a tontine. The tontine was a failure, as only about £100,000 was subscribed. Then Montagu quickly changed the terms of the loan by converting it into a life annuity. The terms of the latter were more favorably received and subscriptions totaling almost £800,000 were obtained.

The year 1694 found Montagu faced with the problem of raising a loan of £2,000,000 to provide for the deficiency in a £5,000,000 expenditure program. He decided upon a plan to borrow by means of a fixed-term annuity. The plan met with little response. To make it more attractive, Montagu converted the loan into a lottery: £40,000 was to be divided yearly among the subscribers who drew the lucky numbers. The lottery was more successful. But Montagu's problems were only partially solved, as the lottery provided for only one-half of the $2,000,-000 deficiency.

Paterson's Bank Scheme. — Being in need of an additional £1,000,-000, Montagu, who had run out of ideas of his own to raise money, now turned to the imagination of his countrymen. Montagu lived in an opportune period in English history for being deluged with schemes for raising money, as the imaginative powers of Englishmen had never been greater. Beginning in the reign of Charles II, there had been an outburst of pamphlets, schemes, and projects that proposed everything from perpetual motion machines to a plan that included the abolishing of taxes. The first few years after the Glorious Revolution witnessed an upturn in the passion for speculation. It was the era of company-forming and stockjobbing. Private lotteries were enjoying a great popularity. The environment was right for producing something revolutionary in public finance.

Montagu considered over seventy financial schemes before he decided upon a proposal submitted by William Paterson, who was one of the more famous projectors and adventurers of that speculative age. The scheme selected by Montagu was that, in return for a loan of £1,200,000, the subscribers would receive an annual interest payment of £100,000, and be formed into a corporation with exclusive banking privileges. New duties on tonnage were to be levied to pay the annuity. No provision was to be made for principal. The government reserved the right, however, to refuse to renew the charter, which was to be granted for twelve years, and to terminate the loan by paying off the debt in a lump sum.

The bank scheme of 1694 was a complete success. The organization of the loan proceeded quickly; the subscribers to the Bank of England totaled about 1,300 in number and were composed primarily of London businessmen, merchants, and companies. The exuberant optimism of the day, combined with a scheme which had Parliamentary backing and a guaranteed income from taxes, explain the fact that the whole £1,200,000 was subscribed within twelve days.

Montagu had known of this bank scheme for several years. On repeated occasions since 1691, Paterson had tried to obtain approval of his project for a Bank of England. None of the earlier proposals, however, had met with any success. But now the project appeared to be a relatively inexpensive method of contracting a loan, and the political opposition to the bank was not able to maintain its strength in face of

13

the urgency for funds prevailing in 1694.[1] A leading historian of the bank has said: "The project was only passed because the Government needed the money and could not obtain it otherwise."[2] The judgment of still another investigator is that the bank was "chartered by the Government as a money-raising machine."[3]

Beginning of the Funding System. — The debt created by the Bank of England scheme in 1694 marks the beginning of the English funding system. The bank debt filled the requirements of a funded debt: taxes were permanently pledged for the payment of interest, and no provision was simultaneously made with the creditors to reimburse the principal. Since the bank's charter was continually being renewed, the government never exercised its right to pay off the principal.

The element of perpetuity was an essential part of what was understood by the term "funded debt" in England throughout the eighteenth century.[4] Montagu's new system of borrowing had not been perfected with the lottery and tontine loans, because some provision for the payment of principal was still, in effect, being made, though in installments. The loans of 1692 were transitional debt forms between an anticipation system and a funding system. The origin of the funded debt and the Bank of England, therefore, would seem to coincide. The bank loan placed the entire aim of debt service on the payment of interest only. The revolutionary expedient of perpetual borrowing had begun.

INCORPORATION OF DEBT IN THE PRIVILEGED COMPANIES

The Bank of England scheme was the beginning of the practice of financing government through privileged companies. In order to obtain new sources of borrowing, or to exploit the old sources, the government had to continue granting banking and trading privileges. The necessity of offering special inducements to the public creditors is evidence of the fact that the funded debt in England was born in an age of low public credit. The debt had to grow, of course, because of the government's continued high expenditure and low tax policies.

1. The opposition was composed of several factions. The Tories, of course, opposed a bank because they were afraid it would strengthen the government. The goldsmiths, dissident Whigs, and rival schemers produced additional arguments against the bank.

2. A. Andreades, *History of the Bank of England,* trans. Christabel Meredith (2d ed.; London: P. S. King and Sons, Ltd., 1924), p. 70.

3. Sir John Harold Clapham, *The Bank of England, a History* (New York: The Macmillan Co., 1945), I, 24.

4. Adam Smith, *Wealth of Nations,* ed. Edwin Cannan (New York: The Modern Library, 1937), p. 865.

East India Company. — In 1698, when financial difficulties again had arisen, the government promised that the rights of incorporation and special trading privileges would be given to any group of persons who would advance £2,000,000 to the government. Taxes were levied and pledged for the payment of interest at a rate of 8 per cent. The East India Company, which was having internal difficulties, did not respond to the offer, but a group endeavoring to organize a new East India Company did. The subscriptions were quickly filled and the project became a complete success.

Another feature of the practice of raising loans by the creation of privileged corporations was that the corporation's service to the government did not cease with its creation. In 1708, the East India Company, which by this time had united with the old company, lent £1,200,000 to the government. An additional £1,000,000 was advanced to the government in 1743. It was the last of the permanent advances made by this company to the government. However, the East India Company was also used by the government as a source of short-term advances.

South Sea Company. — The principle of incorporating debt reached its high point with the South Sea Company. By 1711 the floating debt had reached a state where it had become a major problem. The bulk of the floating debt had continued to be secured by the system of anticipation. The earmarking of taxes had led to the security of some debt holders, but to the insecurity of the whole floating debt. The different due dates, the different rates of interest, and the different revenues pledged — some with surpluses and some with deficits — had placed the unfunded portion of the debt in a state of confusion. It was decided, therefore, to consolidate the entire floating debt and to convert it into a debt bearing interest only, but repayable at the government's will. The floating debt would then become a funded debt. Special corporate privileges were offered to any group of persons who would help the government accomplish this funding of the floating debt, and this offer gave birth to the South Sea Company. In return for what amounted to a loan to the government of £9,177,967, the subscribers were incorporated and granted exclusive trading rights in certain areas of the world. The transaction was actually accomplished on the basis of exchanging old debt for the new corporate stock. The taxes on which the floating debt had been secured were made perpetual, and pledged for the payment of interest on the loan at a rate of 6 per cent. The subscriptions were quickly filled, and the South Sea Company got off to a successful start.

15

The scheme proposed by the South Sea Company in 1720 is the most famous event of that company's history. The company's proposal to the government at that time was to convert the entire English public debt of £30,981,712 into a debt held by the company. Subscriptions would be sold, payable either in old debt or in money, in order to acquire or purchase all the debt, including that held by the Bank of England and the East India Company. The company's offer was tempting to the government as it included a plan to lower the rate of interest from the existing rate to 5 per cent, until 1727, and 4 per cent thereafter. The Bank of England, on hearing of the proposition, retaliated by asking the government to give the bank the exclusive right to fulfill the same plan. After the Bank of England's counterproposal became known, the South Sea Company offered the government a cash bonus of £3,500,000 for the sole right to carry out the project. The bank came back with a bonus offer of £5,000,000. The South Sea Company was finally awarded the project, but not until it offered £7,500,000.

The Company's stock then began to soar in price, having gone from £100 per share to £2,000. Rumors were spread that the company had discovered new markets, rich mines, and hidden treasures that would make its stockholders fabulously rich. The South Sea Company's success touched off another rage of schemes and projects which spread throughout England. Subscriptions were sold even by promoters whose projects were held secret from the subscribers.

The South Sea Company, fearing that the rage of schemes (known as the bubble companies) would bring on its own collapse, successfully pleaded with the government to pass legislation dissolving these new companies. The Bubble Act, which was passed within that year, 1720, brought a quick downfall of the bubble companies.

The South Sea Company narrowly escaped witnessing its own collapse. Although the company survived, it was only partly successful in accomplishing its objective, for it never did take over the debt held by the Bank of England and the East India Company, although it did succeed in obtaining the bulk of the remaining debt. Its exclusive trading privileges turned out to be of little value. It became a company concerned only with the holding and managing of a part of the public debt.

The South Sea Company marks the last phase of the era in which the government borrowed chiefly by the creation of privileged companies. There were four other instances, including two abortive attempts, of the creation of companies for the incorporation of debt. Subsequent borrowing by the English government was based more on direct appeals to the public and the expansion of both the funded and unfunded debt holdings of the Bank of England.

CHANGING DEBT POLICIES AND GROWTH OF THE NATIONAL DEBT

From the revolution to 1697, the year in which the war with Louis XIV ended, the English national debt had grown from £664,263 to £21,515,742, the greater portion of which was still of a floating character. Queen Anne's war, which lasted from 1702 to 1713, brought the debt to £52,145,363. Money was borrowed during the war by annuities, lotteries, and loans from the companies. By 1714 the funded debt had become predominant, a fact which made the greater part of the debt perpetual — the creditor could not demand his money.

All annuities sold to the public were either life, term, or tontine annuities. These were collectively called the terminable annuities. The only perpetual or permanent annuities outstanding were the funded debts held by the three companies. A change in policy occurred in 1714, from which time perpetual annuities were sold directly to the public, rather than being exclusively incorporated in the privileged companies. The sale of these perpetual annuities to the public marked the beginning of the decline of the relative importance of borrowing either through the companies or by terminable annuities.

Another series of English wars came to an end in 1748. The total debt stood at £79,293,713. The government's debt to the three companies was still a major component of the national debt, but the policy of borrowing on perpetual annuities sold directly to the public had increased tremendously. The debt to the companies, however, did not increase in the same proportion. The funded debt totaled £69,797,904, of which £11,686,000 was held by the Bank of England; £4,200,000 was held by the East India Company; and £27,302,205 was held by the South Sea Company. The perpetual annuities held by the public amounted to £25,609,701.

At the end of the Seven Years' War the total English debt was £138,865,430. Twenty years later, in 1783, the American war had caused the debt to reach £249,851,628.

England did not enter another war until 1793. During the ten years of peace the most important development in English fiscal policies was Pitt's sinking fund. Another of Pitt's actions during this time was the funding of almost £16,200,000 of floating debt in 1784; and in 1789 he also employed a tontine loan. But in 1793 war with France broke out, and by 1795 the funded debt alone had climbed to £297,391,899.

17

3. ENGLISH FISCAL POLICIES: THE SINKING FUND

The English funding system, including the Bank of England and the other privileged companies through which the debt was incorporated, originated and grew as a response to a series of national crises. Its sole purpose was to provide a vast reservoir of revenue to finance governmental expenditures. From its small beginning in 1694, Montagu's new system of borrowing was repeatedly employed throughout the eighteenth century as the simplest solution to each emergency that suddenly developed. After each emergency had been met and passed, the renewed reliance on the funding system left its mark by another privileged company, or the extended monopoly rights of the old companies, or additional public creditors. In any case, the result was a larger outstanding debt, which made additional burdens on the funds or taxes mortgaged to pay the interest. In short, the problem of a large national debt had been created. Just as the rise of the national state had transferred the revenue problem from the king to the nation, so the policy of borrowing had created a national instead of a personal debt. During this transitional period, in which financial problems were becoming problems of public instead of private finance, it would be too much to expect a corresponding shift in analysis. The policy of incorporating debt into the privileged companies as a method of conducting a funding system was in part due to this failure to perceive the powers the sovereign state possessed. Just as the king had gone to the goldsmiths in an emergency, so the new nation thought it had to create a chain of super-goldsmith syndicates, namely, the East India Company, the South Sea Company, and the Bank of England. This outlook was carried into the handling of the problem created by the national debt. Assuming that a debt was capable of bankrupting a nation as well as a person, the statesmen thought it imperative to extinguish the debt. The similarity in handling the debt problem was that England again looked to a power outside the state to solve its debt payment problem. A scheme was needed — and the answer was found in the magic of a sinking fund. It must be added, however, that the sinking fund policy represented a stage in fiscal policy history when a distinction was beginning to be made between private and public finance. The sinking fund, as will be seen, rested on the assumption that the state, and only the state, could borrow at simple interest to pay off debt at compound interest. Statesmen only dimly realized that different principles were involved in public finance. Their inability to identify those principles produced one of the greatest fiascoes in financial history.

WALPOLE'S SINKING FUND

During the period of peace which began in 1713, there were many proposals for discharging the national debt.[1] In 1714, Archibald Hutcheson proposed a plan for paying off the debt in one stroke — by means of a levy on property. Another proposal was made by Sir Humphrey Mackworth, who suggested that the debt could be quickly paid by printing paper money and issuing it to the government's creditors. Proposals to repay the debt gradually by means of taxation or economy in expenditures were not products of this period in English history. The English mind of the time was more prone to schemes of a sensational or magical quality.

By 1715 when Sir Robert Walpole became Chancellor of the Exchequer, the national debt had grown to over £50,000,000. Walpole requested William Paterson, the founder of the Bank of England, to work out a scheme of debt redemption. Paterson produced calculations showing how a sinking fund arrangement could free the government of debt in twenty-two years, but before Walpole could carry out this plan, a change in government occurred, and Stanhope replaced Walpole as Chancellor of the Exchequer. Rather than abandoning Walpole's plan, however, Stanhope became the executor of the sinking fund.

Mechanics and Principles of Debt Redemption. — The act of 1716, which established the sinking fund, first provided for a reorganization of the system of pledging taxes for servicing the interest on the funded debt. Four funds were created: the aggregate fund, the South Sea fund, the general fund, and the sinking fund. All outstanding debts were now to receive their interest payments from one of the first three funds, to which the various taxes were assigned and pledged perpetually. The fourth fund, the sinking fund, had as its source of income all surpluses that arose in the first three funds. Such surpluses would arise if

1. E. L. Hargreaves, *The National Debt* (London: Edward Arnold and Co., 1930), pp. 30-37.

the interest payments charged to the funds were less than the yield of the taxes assigned to the funds.

The act then called for the inviolable application of the income of the sinking fund to the purchase and redemption of debt incurred prior to 1717. The annual redemption of debt would have the effect of decreasing the interest payments charged to the first three funds, thus annually increasing their surpluses, which was the equivalent of increasing the annual income of the sinking fund.

History and Operation of the Fund. — The problem confronting Stanhope, the Chancellor of the Exchequer, was that of increasing the surpluses of the aggregate, South Sea, and general funds. The means of obtaining surpluses in the three funds hinged on the possibility of converting the debt to a lower rate of interest. In 1714, the legal rate of interest had been reduced from 6 per cent to 5 per cent. Since the national debt bore a 6 per cent rate or more, a possibility existed that a reduction was feasible at this time. Under threat of being paid off, the bondholders would be asked to renegotiate interest rates to a lower level.

The conversion of 1717 was a complete success. The bank and the South Sea Company agreed to a reduction of interest from 6 per cent to 5 per cent. Stanhope had thus provided a surplus to feed the sinking fund. When Walpole again came to power in 1727, he was able to make another conversion operation on the debts held by the bank and the South Sea Company, by reducing to 4 per cent the interest rate on this segment of the debt.

The sinking fund's history became a series of encroachments on its income, and the idea of an inviolable application of the sinking fund was being abandoned. In 1733 Walpole raided the sinking fund by using £500,000 of its income for current services. Two years previously he had reduced the land tax from four shillings on the pound to one shilling. His motive, it has been said, was to bring the landed men into the support of the Hanoverian government.[2] In 1733, therefore, he preferred raiding his sinking fund to restoring the former level of the land tax. Walpole again used the sinking fund for current services in 1734, this time withdrawing £1,200,000 of its income. In 1735, Walpole borrowed by mortgaging the sinking fund's entire income. After 1752, Walpole's sinking fund ceased operating in a debt redeeming capacity, and became diverted to other purposes.

2. John Morley, *Walpole* (London: Macmillan and Co., Ltd., 1930), p. 180.

The sinking fund of 1716 found its theoretician in Sir Nathaniel Gould. Writing in 1726, one year before the sinking fund's income would become a target for raids by Walpole, Gould said: "The present Sinking Fund is an Expedient, from which we may with great Confidence expect the full and effectual Payment of the Principal of our present Debts within a few Years." Gould's immediate purpose in writing was the prevailing "Suspicion of the Inefficiency of this Provision."[3] It was even being said that the national debt had increased since the sinking fund's establishment. Gould branded this assertion untrue, and reasoned that new borrowings were sufficiently smaller than old debt redeemed by the sinking fund to produce a £2,000,000 net reduction in the national debt.

Gould explained the basis of his confidence in the sinking fund's ability to bring about a speedy liquidation of the national debt. He produced calculations to show that a sinking fund, starting with an income from the surpluses of the three funds of £1,000,000, would liquidate a debt of £50,000,000 bearing 4 per cent interest in twenty-eight years. Gould pointed out that this and similar calculations were based on the principle that "the annual Income of the Sinking Fund . . . increases yearly in the same manner and Proportion as a Principal sum put out and continued at compound Interest."[4]

The Concept of a Perpetual Debt

After the sinking fund had become diverted from its original purpose, a new attitude towards national debts arose in England. Previously, English thought on national debts was characterized by a determination to pay off the debt. Since the sinking fund had become discredited, few proposals advocating the payment of the debt were forthcoming. The main emphasis was now on the prevention of further increases in the debt. The result was the rise of the concept of a perpetual debt, because the permanent existence of the debt was coming to be regarded as inevitable.

The realization that England had a large national debt that could not be removed by the crank of the printing press or the powers of a sinking fund produced pessimistic debt philosophies. Adam Smith can be classified as one of the pessimists of the period. He gave support to

3. *An Essay on the Publick Debts of This Kingdom* (London: J. Peele, 1726), pp. 7, 62.
4. *Ibid.*, p. 22.

bankruptcy fears when he said that national debts "at present oppress, and will in the long-run probably ruin, all the great nations of Europe." The evil was the funding system, that is, the mortgaging of taxes in perpetuity for the payment of only the interest on debt.[5] The Bank of England debt was the beginning of the funding system, and this "ruinous practice" was later extended to loans made directly from the public. The practice was entered into because it permitted the raising of the largest sums possible for the smallest increase in taxes.

Smith had absolutely no faith in a sinking fund. The income of a sinking fund was either too small, or, if it was of significant size, it was always diverted to purposes other than debt redemption. In fact, Smith argued a sinking fund tends to increase debt:

> A sinking fund, though instituted for the payment of old, facilitates very much the contracting of new debts. It is a subsidiary fund always at hand to be mortgaged in aid of any other doubtful fund, upon which money is proposed to be raised in any exigency of the state.[6]

Smith could see no possibility, at least under the conditions of 1776, for any debt reduction obtained by any means. His outlook was thoroughly pessimistic, for experience had proven that "when national debts had once been accumulated to a certain degree, there is scarce . . . a single instance of their having been fairly and completely paid."[7]

Dr. Richard Price and Rediscovery of Powers of a Sinking Fund

Just when most Englishmen were learning to accept the existence of a permanent debt, Dr. Richard Price, a Nonconformist minister, stirred the nation by his agitation for the re-establishment of a sinking fund. His writings on the national debt, which date from 1771, became more widely read than any other work on that subject in the eighteenth century.[8] Dr. Price had rediscovered that, if certain principles were rigidly followed, a sinking fund had properties that enabled it to "discharge the *largest* debt that a State could have occasion to contract, at a *small* expense, and in as little time as its interest could possibly require."[9] Actually, Dr. Price contributed little that was new. Nathaniel

5. Smith, pp. 863, 865.
6. *Ibid.*, p. 868.　　　　　　　　　　　　　　　　7. *Ibid.*, p. 882.
8. Carl B. Cone, *Torchbearer of Freedom: The Influence of Richard Price on Eighteenth Century Thought* (Lexington: University of Kentucky, 1952), p. 135.
9. *An Appeal to the Public on the Subject of the National Debt* (London: T. Cadell, 1772), p. 40.

22

Gould had expressed essentially the same ideas forty-five years before. Perhaps the mood of England was more opportune for Dr. Price: frightened by the existence of a perpetual debt, his countrymen might have seen one more chance to rid the nation of that financial monster created by a funding system. In any event, England rallied to the doctor's crusade. Fifteen years after he had first published his ideas, Dr. Price's sinking fund became law.

Debt and Depopulation. — Although Dr. Price was a minister, he preferred other pursuits, especially those of the political philosopher, mathematician, demographer, and financier. In 1765, after tabulating the returns of the window-tax surveyors, Dr. Price found the facts to be worse than he had imagined: the population of England had declined by 30 per cent[10] since the revolution.[11] He concluded that the large national debt not only was responsible for placing England in a near state of bankruptcy, but it was also the cause of "that DEPOPULATION which has been going on among us, ever since it began."[12] The taxes which had been levied to pay the interest on the debt had doubled the price of articles of consumption. These high prices had increased the difficulty of raising a family and, therefore, had discouraged marriage. If the debt were not quickly and drastically reduced England would lose its "trade, liberties, and being as a State."[13]

The Compound-Interest Principle. — To solve the problem of depopulation, Dr. Price insisted that the national debt be extinguished. His solution was the restoration of the sinking fund. He dramatically illustrated the powers of a sinking fund, based on the compound-interest principle, by the following calculation:

> Money bearing compound interest increases at first slowly. But, the rate of increase being continually accelerated, it becomes in some time so rapid, as to mock all the powers of the imagination. One *penny*, put out at our Saviour's birth to 5 per cent, *compound* interest, would, before this time, have increased to a greater sum, than would be contained in *a hundred and fifty millions of earths*, all solid gold. But if put out to *simple* interest, it would, in the same time, have amounted to no more than *seven shillings* and *four pence half-penny*.[14]

10. Dr. Price's assumed direct relationship between the number of people and the number of windows failed to take into consideration the distortion of English architecture resulting from the window tax.

11. Robert L. Heilbroner, *The Wordly Philosophers* (New York: Simon and Schuster, 1953), p. 68.   12. Price, p. 44.   13. *Ibid.*, pp. 46-47.   14. *Ibid.*, p. 19.

23

Applied to debt redemption, the compound-interest principle would produce a sinking fund capable of expunging a national debt of any size, according to Dr. Price.

Dr. Price computed the powers of a sinking fund based on setting apart an annual sum of only £200,000.[15] If the debt purchased bore an interest of 5 per cent, then in the first year the sinking fund would discharge from the public an annuity of £10,000. If, instead of being spent on current services, the annuity were added to the basic income of the sinking fund, and if both were employed in purchasing debt, then an annuity of £10,500 would be disengaged the second year, and the total annual income of the sinking fund would then be £220,500. The sinking fund of £200,000, together with the sum of the annuities disengaged, would increase faster and faster every year, until, in 14 years, the total fund would become £395,866; and in 86 years it would become £13,283,000, Dr. Price calculated.

Dr. Price's example included the assumption that the entire period of 86 years was a period of budget deficits. His specific figure was that the government had to borrow £3,000,000 every year. But the sinking fund, which had grown to £13,283,000, had paid off almost £262,000,000 of debt in the 86 years. According to his model, therefore, the powers of a £200,000 sinking fund more than compensated for the large yearly borrowings:

> And, consequently, it appears, that though the State had been all along adding every year to its debt three millions; that is, though in the time supposed it had contracted a debt of 258 millions, it would have been more than discharged, at no greater expense than an annual saving of £200,000.[16]

Dr. Price analyzed Walpole's sinking fund and found that it worked on the compound-interest basis until the principle of an inviolable application of a sinking fund's income to the payment of debt was abandoned. If it had continued to operate without a diversion of its income, it would have left England tax-free and with a great treasure.[17] Dr. Price believed that the government knew of the powers of the sinking fund but purposely had abandoned it, because "the loss, thereof, of the *dependence* created by the National Debt, and of the security it gave to the *Hanoverian* succession and the administration, was brought in too near view."[18]

15. *Ibid.*, pp. 4-7.   16. *Ibid.*, pp. 5-6.
17. *Ibid.*, p. 37.   18. *Ibid.*, p. 38.

Dr. Price attacked the justification that had been made for the encroachments on Walpole's sinking fund — the idea that it made no difference where money was obtained in an emergency, whether from the sinking fund or from new borrowings. But Dr. Price believed that the difference was no less than infinite:

> When a State borrows, it pays . . . only *simple* interest for money. When it alienates a Fund appropriated to the payment of its debts, it loses the advantage of money, that would have been otherwise improved necessarily at *compound* interest.[19]

The "barbarous policy" of raiding the sinking fund had cost the kingdom millions of pounds, Dr. Price thought, and had seriously delayed the day when the national debt would be paid and all taxes annihilated.

Principles Emphasized. — Dr. Price emphasized certain principles which Gould had either lightly treated or merely implied. These principles were (1) borrowing to maintain a sinking fund, (2) contracting national debts at a high rate of interest, (3) maintaining a sinking fund during war, and (4) the establishment of special commissioners to manage the sinking fund.

Dr. Price emphasized that the sinking fund's income need not be derived from decreased expenditures, increased taxes, or even a conversion of the debt to a lower rate of interest:

> A State may, without difficulty, redeem all its debts by borrowing money for that purpose, at an equal or even any higher interest than the debt bears; and, without providing any other Funds than such small ones, as shall from year to year become necessary to pay the interest of the sums borrowed.[20]

Dr. Price admitted that the contracting of new debt to redeem old debt may have the appearance of being self-defeating:

> In *private life*, such a measure would be justly deemed absurd. But in a *State* it would be the effect of the soundest policy.[21]

His discovery was that the state could pursue such a policy because of its unique powers:

> Every such measure . . . is only a course of borrowing sums at

19. *Ibid.*, p. 13.
20. *Ibid.*, pp. 15-16.
21. *Ibid.*, p. 16.

simple interest, in order to improve them at *compound* interest. And as the benefits hence arising become in time infinite, THERE IS NOTHING THAT A STATE MAY NOT DO BY IT.[22]

Since taxes would have to be levied to pay the interest on the sums borrowed, Dr. Price recommended for this purpose a tax on celibacy, a tax which would stimulate population growth while removing the cause of depopulation, the national debt.

It might be noted that Dr. Price gave only slight recognition to the necessity of levying taxes for the payment of debt. His entire emphasis was on borrowing, not on taxation. Robert Hamilton has summarized these points emphasized by Dr. Price and their implication for tax policy:

> The doctrine maintained by Dr. Price is that the formation and inviolable appropriation of a sinking fund, operating by compound interest, *in war as well as in peace*, is a measure of the utmost consequence, and that the effects of this system are greatly superior to those of any other application of a surplus, *the expenditure and taxation* being *equal*. His work means this, or it means nothing: for it was never called in question that saving of expenditure, or increase of taxation, have a powerful effect on the state of the national finances.[23]

A second principle emphasized by Dr. Price was that a sinking fund based on the compound-interest principle would redeem a given debt faster if the debt bore a high, rather than a low, rate of interest.[24] The best conversion policy, therefore, was to convert the national debt from a low to a higher rate of interest.

Dr. Price emphasized that the sinking fund should never be suspended during war.[25] In fact, war might even accelerate the redemption of debt, because of a possible rise in the rate of interest. Its suspension would prevent the sinking fund from obtaining the full accumulative effect of a sum growing at compound interest. The two periods of peace interrupted by a war should be united by the continued operation of the sinking fund.

Finally, Dr. Price also emphasized the creation of special commissioners to manage the sinking fund. Dr. Price's proposal was that the income of the sinking fund was to be conceived not as being applied

22. *Ibid.*, pp. 41-42.
23. *An Inquiry Concerning . . . the National Debt* (3d ed.; Edinburgh: Oliphant, Waugh, and Innes, 1818), pp. 181-82.
24. Price, pp. 40-42. 25. *Ibid.*, pp. 17-18, 43.

directly to debt, but as being invested in active government securities destined to redeem the debt at some later date — when the total amount of securities held by the commissioners was equal to the total amount of the public debt. In short, the securities invested in were precisely the same securities that were to be paid off. Since the debt purchased was not initially canceled, the legal fiction arises that the commissioners would be creditors of the government. The nominal debt and the nominal interest charges remain the same throughout the period of debt redemption. When the debt purchased by the commissioners became equal to the nominal debt, then the former would be canceled, and the national debt would drop to zero.

The foundation for the rise of a great financial delusion was laid by the acceptance of Dr. Price's ideas. Even if the sinking fund of the Walpole-Stanhope era had not produced any gross misconceptions about the powers of a sinking fund, it was certain that such would emerge out of the propagandizing of Dr. Price. The mere change in order of public accounts entailed by the creation of special sinking fund commissioners was interpreted as involving a superiority over the previous arrangement. The change in form of the sinking fund became associated with the belief in the unique ability of the government to borrow at simple interest in order to pay off debt at compound interest.

It is indeed possible that the paying off of a public debt could take place at a rate describable by compound-interest calculations. This could be true for a private debt as well. But the time required to discharge a debt would be the same, assuming an equal excess of revenues over expenditures, whether the debt is canceled upon purchase from the public creditors, or accumulated as active stock to the credit of sinking fund commissioners. In the first case, the reduction in the required interest payments will, by increasing the government's surplus, permit an increasing amount of debt to be extinguished annually. And in the second case, the sinking fund commissioners would buy increasing amounts of stock by a rate of increase equal to the increased interest earnings of the holdings of the sinking fund. The latter case only complicates the process of achieving the same results.

Dr. Price's discovery was that the state could borrow money at simple interest and improve it at compound interest. It appeared to him that a state had the unique ability to do what an individual could not do, because Dr. Price had built into his model taxes which were equal to the interest on the sums borrowed. Additional taxation, with or without a sinking fund, can accelerate by compound interest the discharge of a public debt, if it is in the process of redemption. When Dr. Price stated that a debt of £258,000,000 could be paid off in 86 years at no greater expense than an annual saving of £200,000, he overlooked the taxes imposed year after year to pay the interest on the new sums borrowed. Failing to emphasize this assumption of his model, he and others after him failed to recognize explicitly the importance of taxation in the extinction of debt through a sinking fund.

If a period of peace is ended by war, and budget surpluses turn into deficits, it makes no difference whether the period of peace following the war is linked to the period of peace preceding the war by the continued operation of a sinking fund. When the deficits begin, debt retirement ends. The postwar efforts to extinguish debt begin on a new basis, and in no way can they be united to the prewar basis of discharging debt to obtain the powerful effect from the long continuance of compound interest. All the efforts to achieve other results by the interposition of sinking fund commissioners would be of no avail. Debt cannot be placed into the process of being discharged as long as a period of deficits exists.

The idea of converting the debt to a high rate of interest in order to speed the process of debt payment is without foundation. To engage in such a policy, a state would have to increase taxes by the amount necessary to pay the higher rate of interest in order merely to prevent further accumulation of debt or to slow down the retirement of debt. While it is true that a sum reaches a given magnitude sooner when compounded at a higher interest rate, it is also true that the accumulation of debt would progress at the same rate unless new taxes are levied.

Dr. Price failed to see that it was the higher taxation associated with his conversion plan, not the higher interest rate in itself, that accelerated debt reduction. In any situation, the amount of outstanding debt remaining after a given period during which a sinking fund operates is, at best, the same as the amount of debt remaining under equal expenditures and taxation when no sinking fund commissioners had to borrow at a high rate of interest to purchase debt bearing a smaller rate of interest. But even if borrowing took place at the same rate of interest, the expenses connected with borrowing and purchasing operations would make the sinking fund method produce poorer results.

PITT'S SINKING FUND

William Pitt's rise to power in 1783 turned out to be a very pleasing event for Dr. Price.[26] On taking office, Pitt not only planned to introduce reforms in taxation and economy in expenditures, both of which were later accomplished, but he also planned to introduce a scheme for the payment of the debt.[27] In regard to the latter of his plans, Pitt wrote to a friend in 1785: "I am half mad with a project which will give our supplies the effect almost of magic in the reduction of debt."[28] The young Prime Minister was obviously a convert to the wave of optimism that had grown up since Dr. Price had published his calculations on the powers of a sinking fund based on the compound-interest principle.

Establishment. — Pitt began ordering the finances of the country in a manner that would be favorable to a sinking fund's future establishment. The reforms in the tax and expenditure policies introduced were responsible for the surplus of revenue over expenditures that developed in 1786. Pitt was also contemplating a conversion of the debt to a higher rate of interest, an expedient that Dr. Price had urged to accelerate the powers of a sinking fund. Pitt made a speech in 1784, in which he said:

> It was always my idea that a fund [i.e., funded debt] at a high rate of interest is better to the country than those at low rates; that a four per cent. is preferable to a three per cent., and a five per cent. better than a four. The reason is that in all operations of finance we should always have in view a plan of redemption. Gradually to redeem and to extinguish our debt ought ever to be the wise pursuit of Government. Every scheme and operation of finance should be directed to that end, and managed with that view.[29]

Early in 1786, Pitt wrote a letter to Dr. Price, informing him that the situation of the revenue was now right for the establishment of a sinking fund.[30] Pitt enclosed an outline of a sinking fund plan, and a conversion scheme to accompany it. He planned to convert £107,000,000 of 3 per cent debt to 5 per cent debt. Pitt then asked Dr. Price to make comments and suggestions for improvements.

Eleven days later, Dr. Price, being extremely concerned over the matter, went to Pitt in person. He objected to parts of Pitt's plan, including some of the details on the conversion scheme. Dr. Price then

---

26. Pitt was Prime Minister from 1783 to 1801, and again from 1804 to 1806. He was only twenty-four years of age in 1783.
27. Sydney Buxton, *Finance and Politics* (London: John Murray, 1888), I, 3.
28. Quoted in Cone, p. 141.
29. *Ibid.*, p. 142.
30. Hargreaves, p. 99. See also Cone, p. 143.

proposed three alternative plans for a sinking fund, and Pitt asked that the plans be drawn up in detail.

Pitt rejected two of the plans, because they called for an increase in taxation. If possible, he wanted to avoid any further tax increases. Pitt then drew up and sent to Parliament a bill that was based on Dr. Price's remaining plan.

The sinking fund bill, which successfully passed through Parliament, had several important features. The revenues, which in 1716 had become assigned to the aggregate, South Sea, and general funds, were united and assigned to one fund, the consolidated fund, which was pledged to the public creditors for the payment of interest on the debt. A permanent annual appropriation of £1,000,000 from the consolidated fund was to be turned over to the Board of Commissioners of the Sinking Fund, a permanent branch of administration created by Pitt to prevent raids on the sinking fund's income. The commissioners were to apply the £1,000,000 appropriation to the purchase of funded debt at market prices, whether at, above, or below par. The debt purchased was not to be canceled; it would still bear interest. On their expiration, the terminable annuities were also to continue to bear interest to the credit of the sinking fund. The commissioners were to make purchases of debt for the sinking fund with the income from all sources — the permanent appropriation, the interest on the funded debt purchased, and the interest on the terminable annuities — until the total income of the sinking fund reached £4,000,000. Thereafter, additional debt purchased by the sinking fund would be canceled. When the sinking fund's holdings of debt, both active and canceled, equaled the total amount of the debt, then the entire debt would be considered paid.

Dr. Price was pleased with Pitt's sinking fund, but he was not entirely satisfied. He especially objected to the provision which would prevent the accumulation of the sinking fund's income from exceeding £4,000,000. This would, of course, prevent the compound-interest principle from exerting its full potential.

Pitt's reason for the £4,000,000 limit is not definitely known. Perhaps he planned for upward adjustments in the legal limit as the existing limit was approached. But probably the real explanation for Pitt's £4,000,000 limit is that Pitt, a disciple of Adam Smith, feared that a sinking fund possessing too large an income would become a target for raids by future governments. Pitt had hoped to establish his fame, not on the sinking fund principle itself, but on the safeguards he had provided to insure the inviolable application of the sinking fund to the purchase of debt. The idea of the creation of the Commissioners of the Sinking Fund was original with Dr. Price, not with Pitt. More important in preventing future raids on the sinking fund was the £4,000,000 limit, because, without this safeguard, the sinking fund would grow to such great size that the temptation to raid it would become overwhelming. Nevertheless, the £4,000,000 limit was completely abolished in 1802, when Pitt was out of office, and it was not restored when Pitt returned to office.

History. — Pitt's sinking fund began in 1786 with an appropriation of £1,000,000 derived from a surplus of revenue over expenditures. By 1793, the sinking fund's income had grown to £1,630,000, mostly because of the accumulated interest on the stock purchased. In 1793 the war with France began. The emerging era of budget deficits was to be a test of how closely Dr. Price's sinking fund theories were being followed. From 1793 to 1801, the year when Pitt left office, the sinking fund was maintained in full operation. Money had to be borrowed to feed the sinking fund, because no surplus of revenue over expenditure existed. In fact, from the beginning of the war until 1828, when the sinking fund was finally abandoned, not one single year passed in which money was not borrowed to maintain the sinking fund. This was not regarded as tragedy, because orthodox opinion regarded it as not merely unavoidable but actually desirable to borrow in order to maintain the sinking fund.[31]

The powers of the sinking fund to purchase debt were even increased during the war. The total annual income of the sinking fund was approaching the £4,000,000 limit. Finally, in 1802, the limit was removed by an act of Parliament, and, being then fully based on the compound-interest principle, the yearly income of the sinking fund climbed to higher and higher levels. The operation of the sinking fund could not, however, make up for the fact that the sums borrowed every year exceeded the debt redeemed.

Buxton has calculated that during the life of the sinking fund, from 1786 to 1828, it redeemed £483,000,000 of funded debt. But during the same period, £1,000,000,000 of funded debt and £50,000,000 of unfunded debt were created. The total net indebtedness, therefore, had gone from approximately £240,000,000 to over £800,000,000. Buxton commented that a great amount of the created debt had "no other pur-

31. Hargreaves, p. 111.

pose than to provide the wherewithal to feed the omnivorous sinking fund."[32]

Contemporary Opinion on its Efficacy. — It is hard to believe the extent to which Englishmen had confidence in the ability of the sinking fund to extinguish debt. Lord Henry Petty, making a speech to Parliament in 1806, said:

> To the consolidated fund the country has looked for the interest of its debt; and for its extinction, to the sinking fund. . . . *It was owing to the institution of the sinking fund that the country was not charged with a much larger amount of debt.* IT WAS AN ADVANTAGE GAINED BY NOTHING.[33]

In 1813, it was proposed that the sinking fund keep in reserve £100,-000,000 or more of purchased debt as a resource in case of war, or as "a treasure as no other country has ever possessed."[34] A fear even developed that the sinking fund was retiring too much debt. The payment of the debt and the abolition of taxes would throw too much money in the economy; inflation and a fall in the rate of interest would be the consequences.

Pitt also was obviously deluded by Dr. Price's sinking fund theories.[35] The letter in which Pitt expressed himself as being "half mad" about the "magic" of a sinking fund and his desire to convert the debt to a higher interest rate clearly indicate that he too was influenced by the compound-interest calculations of Dr. Price. Dr. Price's influence on Pitt is evident from the fact that the sinking fund was maintained inviolably during the war. According to Hargreaves, when Fox criticized the sinking fund scheme as being inalienable during war, "Pitt had replied that this was the great merit of his sinking fund."[36]

The degree to which England had become captivated by the sinking fund has been well expressed by a contemporary of the times:

> An opinion prevails that the minister who instituted the sinking fund has put a powerful machine in action, which, although its first operations were feeble, has now become of great efficacy, and that

---

32. Buxton, I, 216.
33. Quoted in Robert Hamilton, p. 288.
34. *Ibid.*, pp. 232-33.
35. Pitt also accepted Dr. Price's calculations that indicated a 30 per cent decline in the population of England since 1688. He was moved to introduce a poor relief bill designed to stimulate population growth (Heilbroner, p. 68).
36. Hargreaves, p. 101.

the efficacy will continue to increase without any further exertion on our part, like the acceleration of fallen bodies by the power of gravity, till it amount to an indefinite magnitude.[37]

It was not until the same writer, Robert Hamilton, wrote his famous critique of 1813, that the sinking fund became subjected to any serious and widespread criticism.

Writing in 1845, J. R. McCulloch commented that he doubted "whether the history of the world can furnish another instance of so extraordinary an infatuation." "Had the sinking fund involved any unintelligible dogmas," McCulloch continued, "had it addressed itself to popular feelings and passions, or had the notion of its efficacy originated with the mob, the prevalence of the delusion would have been less unaccountable."[38] But since it had been a matter of calculation, he concluded that the captivation of a whole nation by the sinking fund remained, in part, a mystery.

37. Robert Hamilton, p. 202.
38. *A Treatise on the Principles and Practical Influence of Taxation and the Funding System* (London: Longman, Brown, Green, and Longmans, 1845), p. 456.

4. THE AMERICAN PRECEDENTS FOR HAMILTON'S FISCAL POLICIES

In 1789, when Hamilton faced the task of planning his fiscal system, he had a wider choice for its design than is commonly assumed. While it is true that he had no "special training" for the job, he was as well informed on financial subjects as any man of his time. Too, the model for his system could have been based on the fiscal precedents created in America prior to 1789. Hamilton read extensively on economic and financial subjects, and his choice of models could even have been based on present or past precedents established in Holland, France, and other countries. In short, the English imitation thesis assumes a more rigid restraint on his scope of choice than is the case.

The American fiscal policies that could have influenced Hamilton existed more in the thwarted efforts of the Revolutionary government than in actual fiscal policy practice. This is especially true of a funding system and a sinking fund, as these fiscal policies never passed much beyond the stage of being the objects of resolutions of the Continental Congress. The movement to establish a national bank, however, passed beyond the resolution stage and produced an American precedent in the Bank of North America.

The American precedents for Hamilton's fiscal policies were related to the special conditions that grew out of the period of colonial rule and the problems created by financing the Revolution. It will be necessary, therefore, first to examine the pre-Revolutionary history of banking in America, and the financial problems of the Revolution, before going on to the American precedents.

BACKGROUND OF THE AMERICAN FISCAL POLICIES

Although a banking system did not arise in America prior to the late eighteenth century, there were many early proposals and efforts to establish banks of issue based on either land or commodities. Proposals for banks other than specie banks were a reflection of the chronic scarcity of specie in America at this time, for the use of specie in financing imports left little for domestic use. While many colonies required the payment of contracts and taxes in specie, there were instances of colonies making land and commodities legal tender. Barter was not unusual. The chronic shortage of a legal tender and a medium of exchange was felt by the entire economy, including the merchants, agrarians, and colonial governments.

Efforts to establish a private banking system in America virtually ceased in 1741, when Parliament, in order to stop the movements for a land bank, extended the Bubble Act to the American colonies, thus making it impossible to obtain a corporate charter. Efforts to relieve the shortage of money by issuing bills of credit were stopped by another act of Parliament in 1764. Actually, the application of the Bubble Act to the colonies prevented banking only in the incorporated form, since individuals or partnerships could engage in banking. But the effect was to postpone the rise of banking until the colonies had gained their independence and were free to extend corporate privileges. The corporate form was needed because America was not a country with an abundant supply of loanable funds seeking use. The merchants needed to "club together" their scanty funds by means of the corporate form.[1]

Another series of developments that formed part of the background of the Bank of North America was related to the problems encountered in financing the Revolution. The widespread opposition to taxation by a central government made it impractical to levy taxes on the colonists.[2] The outcome was that, during the early years of the Revolution, Congress had to rely principally on printing Continental dollars.

Bills of credit were first issued by Congress in 1775, in the total amount of $6,000,000.[3] The bills circulated at par with specie. The issue of 1776, which amounted to $19,000,000, marks the beginning of the depreciation of the Continental paper money, as the bills circulated at less than 70 per cent of their face value. In 1777 there was emitted an issue totaling $13,000,000, which quickly depreciated all the bills outstanding to about one-third of their face value. The total amount of bills issued each year had to increase to keep pace with the decline in their value. In the same year, the states declared the bills to be legal tender. Then, in 1778, $63,500,000 of the bills were issued. One dollar in paper money was now worth only about twelve cents. In 1779, the large sum of $140,052,000 in bills was issued.

1. Bray Hammond, "Long and Short Term Credit in Early American Banking," *The Quarterly Journal of Economics*, XLIX (November, 1934), 81.
2. Some taxes were levied by the states through the system of requisition.
3. Charles J. Bullock, *The Finances of the United States from 1775 to 1789* (Madison: University of Wisconsin, 1895), pp. 123-36.

By 1780, Congress had issued a total of $241,500,000 in paper money, an amount well above the $200,000,000 limit that Congress had imposed upon its emissions of bills of credit. The value of the paper having dropped to less than two cents on the dollar, this source of financing the war had been exhausted. The legal tender laws, which had caused so much hardship, were abolished in 1780. No effective medium of exchange now existed. All specie was out of circulation. The states, which had themselves issued bills of credit amounting to over $200,000,000, were powerless to help the situation.

Attempts to raise money by domestic loans date from 1776. In that year, Congress authorized that $5,000,000 in bills of credit be borrowed. Loan offices were opened in each state to fill subscriptions. This first effort was met with little response. In the following year, Congress authorized a loan of $15,000,000 which owed its moderate success in part to the higher rate on this loan, 6 per cent instead of 4 per cent. By 1781, when the loan offices were closed, the total amount of Continental paper money borrowed was $67,177,112.

Domestic debt also arose as a result of the issuing of certificates of indebtedness by quartermasters and commissaries for supplies taken by the army. After 1782, it became impossible to pay interest on the loan office certificates and certificates of indebtedness. Indents were issued for the arrearages of interest.

Foreign loans gradually became a significant source of income. Between 1777 and 1783, foreign loans totaled $7,830,517 — $6,352,500 from France; $1,304,000 from Holland; and $174,017 from Spain. After the war, Congress borrowed from Holland to help pay the interest on the foreign debt. New foreign loans of $2,296,000 were contracted for this purpose. However, interest charges on the foreign debt exceeded the loans contracted from Holland by $1,640,071. Again, indents were issued for the arrearages of interest.

In 1777, Congress made the first requisition on the states for money. They were asked to raise $5,000,000 by means of taxes, but, like the requisitions that followed, the response was tardy and inadequate. From 1777 through 1779, total requisitions amounted to $95,000,000 in paper money, but only $54,667,000 was realized from the states. For a short time, beginning in 1780, requisitions were made for specific supplies; for example, so much wheat from each state. The remaining history on the requisitions under the Articles of Confederation showed some signs of improvement, but it also indicated that there were fundamental inadequacies in such a system.

American Precedent for a National Bank

In 1779, America's struggle for independence was threatened by financial difficulties. Congress had almost completely exhausted all of its sources for financing the war. The emissions of paper money had ended in depreciation and had contributed to the decay of commerce and trade. It was under these circumstances and conditions that Alexander Hamilton, a twenty-three-year-old army colonel, produced his first work on finance.

Hamilton's Proposal of 1779. — In a lengthy letter written in 1779 to General John Sullivan, who was a representative of New Hampshire to Congress, Hamilton wrote that "the object of principal concern is the state of our currency."[4] The greater part of commerce, Hamilton said, was being carried on by barter. But Hamilton, unlike most of his contemporaries, believed that depreciation was more than just a problem of an excessive issue of paper money.

Hamilton concurred with the opinion that a foreign loan would help solve the currency problem. The only question was in the manner of employing the loan. It had been suggested that the specie obtained through a foreign loan be used to purchase depreciated money. The remainder of the money, it was argued, would appreciate in value. But Hamilton decided that this employment of the loan would cause only an artificial and temporary appreciation in the Continental money. Moreover, the problem of financing the war would remain, and, since more money would have to be printed to purchase supplies, depreciation would return again.

The fallacy in the plan, according to Hamilton, was that it assumed depreciation was related only to the quantity of money in circulation.[5] The basic reason for the excessive depreciation, Hamilton thought, was the lack of confidence in the money, and merely reducing the quantity of the paper money in circulation would not be of much help. The foreign loan, therefore, needed to be combined with an entirely different sort of plan from those that had been suggested.

"The only plan," wrote Hamilton, "that can preserve the currency is one that will make it the *immediate* interest of the moneyed men to cooperate with government in its support."[6] America, Hamilton continued, was in the same predicament as France had been, prior to the

---

4. *The Works of Alexander Hamilton*, ed. Henry Cabot Lodge (New York: G. P. Putnam's Sons, n.d.), III, 320.

5. *Ibid.*, III, 328. 6. *Ibid.*, III, 332.

Mississippi scheme projected by John Law. France's paper money had also become almost worthless, but the government was powerless by itself to restore the currency, because the people had lost confidence in the government's ability to meet its promises. Law had the insight for a plan to unite the interest and credit of rich individuals with the state. The Banque Generale was created in 1716, with subscriptions for the bank's stock being payable one-fourth in specie and three-fourths in the depreciated paper money.

The foundations of Law's plan were good, Hamilton pointed out, but the superstructure was too vast. The proprietors aimed at unlimited wealth and the government expected too much. But the misuse of Law's plan should not hinder America from adopting its basic principles:

> It will be our wisdom to select what is good in this plan, and in any others that have gone before us, avoiding their defect and excesses. Something on a similar principle in America will alone accomplish the restoration of paper credit, and establish a permanent fund for the future exigencies of government.[7]

Hamilton proposed a plan for an American bank. The bank, to be named the Bank of the United States, was to be created by Congress. Congress would contract a foreign loan of £2,000,000, which would be placed in the bank as part of its stock. This employment of a foreign loan was necessitated by the fact that the American people, unlike the people of France in Law's time, were not able to pay for their bank subscriptions partly in specie, but the public would have to pay for its shares with the depreciated paper money.

The bank plan would accomplish the retirement of the Continental currency. Depreciated bills of credit would be replaced by bank stock and bank notes, the latter being a paper currency that would command the public's confidence. Instead of being based solely on the promises of a weak government, the currency would now be based on the promises of a bank that combined the wealth and credit of both the government and private individuals.

Hamilton's plan also called for changing the monetary unit from the dollar to the pound:

> The denomination of the money is altered; because it will produce a useful illusion. Mankind are much led by sounds and appearances; and the currency having changed its name will seemed to have changed its nature.[8]

---

7. *Ibid.*, III, 333.　　　　　　　　　　　　　　　　8. *Ibid.*, III, 337.

This line of reasoning is typical of Hamilton. When he became Secretary of the Treasury ten years later, he again resorted to proposals that had meaning in their "sounds and appearances."

Hamilton's Proposal of 1780. — Three developments that occurred in 1780 prompted Hamilton to revise his national bank proposal. These developments were the establishment of the Bank of Pennsylvania, the repudiation of the Continental currency, and the improvement in America's specie supply.

In the spring of 1780, a number of citizens of Philadelphia, who deplored the financial distress of the nation, pledged their property and credit "in order to support the credit of a bank to be established for furnishing a supply of provisions for the armies of the United States."[9] Subscriptions of £300,000 quickly began to be filled. The group petitioned Congress to permit them to proceed with their plans to supply the army. On June 21, 1780, Congress accepted the offer. The project was known as the Bank of Pennsylvania.

In 1780, Congress was forced to acknowledge that its source of financing the war through paper emissions had been exhausted. Congress declared, therefore, that the bills were worth only one-fortieth of their face value. They were then made receivable only in payment of a special tax to be levied by the states for the sole purpose of withdrawing the bills from circulation. New bills of credit were to be issued to replace the old bills, but the emission of new bills was to be limited to one-twentieth of the face value of the old bills. Although only $4,000,000 of the new bills were issued, they also quickly depreciated in value. Only $119,400,000 of the old bills were received. The reason was, as usual, the poor compliance of the states. In 1790, there was still outstanding $78,000,000 of the old bills.

Between 1780 and 1783, almost $6,000,000 in specie flowed into America from unexpected sources. The British had flooded New York and other areas with coin while paying their troops and their Tory allies. Also, the French had purchased a considerable amount of supplies in America for their troops with specie. The new conditions precipitated a business boom, and hoarded specie came into circulation.

In September of 1780, Hamilton wrote a letter to James Duane, a representative to Congress from New York, in which he expressed disappointment over the so-called bank that had been formed for the purpose of supplying the army. Hamilton had hoped that it would be "the

9. Lawrence Lewis, Jr., *A History of the Bank of North America* (Philadelphia: J. B. Lippincott and Co., 1882), pp. 18-19.

embryo of a more permanent and extensive establishment."[10] But it was "not conducted on the true principles of a bank." The undertaking would not contribute to solving the currency problem, for it was "a mere subscription of a particular sum of money for a particular purpose."

It was still necessary and urgent, Hamilton felt, to "erect a bank on the joint credit of the public and of individuals."[11] Hamilton's new bank proposal called for some important changes. Subscriptions would no longer be payable in the old bills of credit, because other means had been taken to remove them from circulation. Real property of every kind, including land, would be received in payment of subscriptions. A good landed security would substitute for specie in generating confidence in the new circulating medium. The only qualification was that one-fourth of the subscriptions had to be paid in specie.

Hamilton's Proposal to Robert Morris in 1781. — On February 20, 1781, Robert Morris, a prominent Philadelphia merchant, became Superintendent of Finance. The administration of the nation's finances was now to be conducted by one man instead of by a committee system. Hamilton had been an advocate of the new system and had suggested Morris for the office. On April 30, 1781, having heard of Morris' appointment, Hamilton was inspired to write the Superintendent. The prospects for the establishment of a national bank were now brighter, and Hamilton desired to make his own ideas known to Morris.

In his new bank proposal, Hamilton placed greater emphasis on the problem of improving public credit. For similar purposes, Hamilton pointed out, national banks had been founded in Venice, Genoa, Hamburg, Holland, and England. But England's example "should both persuade and warn us," since England had abused the advantages to be gained from a bank. Hamilton believed that America was more suited to a national bank than England, because:

> 'Tis in republics where banks are most easily established and supported, and where they are least liable to abuse. Our situation will not expose us to frequent wars; and the public will have no temptation to overstrain its credit.[12]

Hamilton also cited the tendency of national banks to stimulate commerce. "Most commercial nations," Hamilton continued, "have found it necessary to institute banks; and they have proved to be the happiest

10. *Works of . . . Hamilton*, I, 233.
11. *Ibid.*, I, 232-33.
12. *Ibid.*, III, 362.

engines that ever were invented for advancing trade." Because of national banks, "industry is increased, commodities are multiplied, agriculture and manufactures flourish; and herein consists the true wealth and prosperity of a state." As for the details of organizing a bank for this purpose, Hamilton concluded, "We shall find good models in the different European banks, which we can accommodate to our circumstances."[13]

The Bank of North America. — On May 17, 1781, seventeen days after Hamilton had written his letter to Morris, Morris submitted to Congress a plan for a national bank. It was read to Congress on May 26. Morris' plan for a Bank of North America called for a national bank with a capital of $400,000.[14] All subscriptions were to be paid in specie. The bank was to be incorporated by Congress and was to receive a monopoly of banking during the war; no state could charter another bank.

On May 26, Morris wrote a reply to Hamilton's letter of April 30. The letter suggested that Morris' bank plan of May 17 was arrived at independently of Hamilton. The Superintendent said:

> It is some time since I received your performance, dated the 30th of April last. I have read it with that attention, which it justly deserves, and finding many parts of it to coincide with my own opinion on the subject, it naturally strengthened that confidence, which every man ought to possess to a certain degree in his own judgment.[15]

However, Morris went on to say that Hamilton's letter made him think about whether he should "interweave a security" in the bank's capital. Hamilton's plan had called for filling subscriptions partly in "good landed security." Morris rejected the idea because it would convey to the public that the bank's paper was circulating on the basis of land, and the foes of the bank might attempt to use this belief to cause a run on the bank.

When Morris' plan was read to Congress a resolution was passed to approve the plan. Before the bank could get started, hostilities ceased with the surrender of the British at Yorktown on October 17, 1781. In the meantime, Morris had contracted a loan from France. He quickly employed $254,000 of specie to subscribe to bank stock on behalf of the

13. *Ibid.*, III, 381.   14. *Journals of the Continental Congress*, XX, 545.
15. Morris to Hamilton, *Diplomatic Correspondence of the Revolution*, ed. Jared Sparks (Boston: Nathan Hale and Gray and Bowen, 1829), XI, 365-66.

United States. The government now owned over half of the bank's stock. On December 31, 1781, Congress passed an ordinance incorporating the bank. The bank finally opened for business on January 7, 1782.

Although the Bank of North America never had the opportunity to become a wartime lending institution to the government, it did extend temporary loans to Congress during the transition to peace. In fact, at the same time that Congress paid for its subscription, it contracted a loan far in excess of the sum subscribed. This financial manipulation had its purpose in obtaining for Congress the desired ownership in the bank's stock.

Because of the bank directors' uneasiness over the extent of the government's loans, Morris began selling the government's stock in the bank in order to repay the loans. In 1783, all of the government's shares had been sold, and in 1784, the government completely repaid all of its loans to the bank.

The Bank of North America began losing the characteristics of a national bank in 1783. The government no longer contracted loans from the bank. After Morris sold the government's bank stock, the government had few direct relations with the bank. No close bond between the bank and the government developed, and the bank's operations became quite local in character.

Because of a fairly widespread belief that Congress did not have the power of incorporation, the Bank of North America petitioned for and received a charter of incorporation from the state of Pennsylvania on April 1, 1782. This was, in effect, an acknowledgment of its dependence on the state of Pennsylvania rather than on the national government.

AMERICAN PRECEDENTS FOR A SINKING FUND AND A FUNDING SYSTEM

Proposals Between 1781 and 1783. — On February 3, 1781, Congress considered a resolution which stated:

> That it is indispensably necessary that the United States in Congress assembled . . . should be vested with the exclusive right of levying duties upon all imported articles.

The purpose of the resolution was to make provision for both the principal and interest of the national debt:

> That the monies arising from the said duties be appropriated to the discharge of the principal and interest of the debts already contracted, or which may be contracted, for supporting the present war.

A qualification was made that Congress "not be empowered to appropriate any duties on imports for perpetual annuities."[16]

The resolution did not gain the unanimous consent of the states necessary to give Congress the taxing power requested. The opponents of the resolution, especially Rhode Island, argued that the proposed tax would bear undue weight on the commercial states and that it would give Congress dangerous powers.

Robert Morris became the champion of the movement to make complete provision for the national debt. He expressed his ideas on the subject rather fully in a letter dated July 29, 1782. After elaborating on his idea that a well-secured national debt would be a cement to the union,[17] he came to the problem at hand, the establishment of the public credit.

The improvement of the public credit, Morris believed, depended on a "solid provision for funding the public debts."[18] He reviewed the efforts made to give Congress the power to levy import duties for this purpose. Morris wanted to supplement this proposed source of revenue with a poll tax, a land tax, and an excise tax on distilled liquors. He wrote:

> I shall now . . . take the liberty to suppose that the revenue I have mentioned . . . were asked for and obtained, as a pledge to the public creditors, to continue until the principal and interest of the debts contracted, or to be contracted, shall be finally paid. . . . I shall further propose, that the surplus of each of these revenues should be carried to a sinking fund.[19]

Morris was thoroughly dedicated to these debt provisions. As Superintendent of Finance he employed all his energy and influence in the establishment of a national revenue, which was the necessary foundation for a funding system and sinking fund.

Upon the recommendation of Morris, a resolution was passed in Congress on December 16, 1782, which, had there been a national revenue, would have established a funding system and a sinking fund in America.

The committee reporting the resolution was headed by Alexander Hamilton, who had first sat in Congress as a delegate from New York on November 25, 1782.[20] The report, which was in Hamilton's hand-

16. *Journals of the Continental Congress*, XIX, 110-13.
17. Morris to the President of Congress, *Diplomatic Correspondence of the Revolution*, XII, 215.
18. *Ibid.*, XII, 220.　　　　　　　　　　　19. *Ibid.*, XII, 232-33.
20. *Journals of the Continental Congress*, XXIII, 750.

writing, began by restating the urgent need for the states to give Congress the power to levy an import duty. Anticipating the fears that Congress was trying to establish a funding system of the English variety, the committee reported:

> The revenue from this duty in the future progress of our trade will afford a surplus beyond the appropriations for interest, which from the express condition of the grant must be applied as a sinking fund to pay off the principal, and by which the supposition of perpetuity is destroyed.[21]

The committee emphasized their debt-repayment intentions by introducing the principle of an inviolable application of the sinking fund's income:

> Whenever the neat produce of any funds recommended by Congress and granted by the states, for funding the debt already contracted, or for procuring future loans for the support of the war, shall exceed the sum requisite for paying the interest on the whole amount of the national debt, . . . the surplus of such grants shall form a sinking fund, to be inviolably appropriated to the payment of the principal of the said debt, and shall on no account be diverted to any other purpose.[22]

The committee reported that an annual provision for the payment of interest was too precarious. By funding the debt, however, national credit would revive and the public creditors would be benefited by having access to their principal through negotiability.

The objectives expressed in the resolution of 1782 must be viewed as only a pre-Constitutional fiscal policy ideal. The resolution was of no value without a national revenue. The stubbornness of Rhode Island and New York in withholding their consent was quickly wrecking the hopes of Morris and his associates.

On April 18, 1783, a resolution was passed that represented a concession to the opposition against a national revenue. It was proposed that the power to levy an import duty be granted to Congress for a term of only twenty-five years.[23]

Morris was furious over the obstructions and the changes being made to his plans. The idea of pledging revenues for a fixed period of time, instead of pledging them permanently until the principal was paid, was

21. *Ibid.*, XXIII, 804.
22. *Ibid.*, XXIII, 809.
23. *Ibid.*, XXIV, 258.

contrary to his conception of a funding program. Morris had informed Congress by letter on January 24, 1783, that he intended to quit his post if more effectual measures were not taken for making provision for the debt.[24] Hamilton also stated that he disliked any plan that made but partial provision for the debt.[25]

CONCLUSIONS ON THE AMERICAN FISCAL POLICY PRECEDENTS

It may be concluded that there were American precedents that could have influenced Alexander Hamilton when he became America's first Secretary of the Treasury. Hamilton definitely had more than two alternatives in constructing his fiscal program in 1790 — instead of inventing new fiscal policies or copying the English, he could have fulfilled the fiscal policy objectives of the pre-Constitutional period.[26]

Inference should not be made that there were no distinctly English ideas circulating in America during this time. On October 6, 1778, for example, a motion was made and passed in Congress to inform Dr. Price that he was now considered a citizen of the United States and that his services were requested in directing the country's finances.[27] Congress was influenced by Dr. Price's ideas on debt redemption and they desired his leadership in establishing a plan to redeem the Continental currency. Dr. Price declined the invitation to come to America and head its finances because of his age and ties in England.[28]

English influences were also evident when Hamilton began planning his financial program. William Bingham, an ardent admirer of English fiscal policies, wrote a letter to Hamilton on November 25, 1789, requesting the newly appointed secretary to adopt policies that could be truly described as imitations of the English models.[29]

Bingham was a Philadelphia merchant, banker, and speculator in land

24. For a detailed analysis of Morris' letter of resignation, including the strategy behind it, see Clarence L. Ver Steeg, *Robert Morris: Revolutionary Financier* (Philadelphia: University of Pennsylvania Press, 1954), pp. 170-73.

25. *Journals of the Continental Congress*, January 29, 1783, XXV, 884.

26. It has been argued that there was no essential difference between the program advocated by Robert Morris and the one finally established by Hamilton. See Ver Steeg, pp. 110, 199.

27. *Journals of the Continental Congress*, XII, 984-85.

28. Price to Franklin, January 18, 1779, *Diplomatic Correspondence of the Revolution*, III, 64.

29. James O. Wettereau, "Letters from Two Business Men to Alexander Hamilton on Federal Fiscal Policy," *Journal of Economic and Business History*, III (1930-1931), 668-82.

and public securities.[30] Being strongly attached to England, he traveled to that country and closely observed Pitt's fiscal policies. It is likely that he believed Pitt's measures were especially suited to the speculative element in America.

Bingham repeatedly suggested in his letter to Hamilton that the English fiscal policies provided the soundest models for imitation. He described the details of Pitt's policies and quoted from English legislation. He advised Hamilton to establish a funding system, a sinking fund, and a national bank. Bingham advocated a sinking fund like Pitt's — one based on a fixed annual appropriation and inviolably applied to debt redemption. His comments on the operation of a sinking fund read like a page from the writings of Dr. Price:

> It is inconceivable what a Progress, a respectable appropriation of Revenue would make in the Diminution of the Debt in a few years, by the operating of compound interest.[31]

There is no question, therefore, that Hamilton entered office with a knowledge not only of the American fiscal policies, which he had helped formulate, but also of the English fiscal policies.[32]

30. All influences and pressures exerted by prominent citizens and associates on Hamilton were not necessarily the efforts of Anglophiles. For an account of some individuals that perhaps influenced Hamilton and for an analysis of the speculation in stock that developed during this period, see the essay on William Duer in Joseph Stancliffe Davis, *Essays in the Earlier History of American Corporations* (Cambridge: Harvard University Press, 1917), I, 111-345.

31. Wettereau, p. 678.

32. It has been recently emphasized by E. P. Panagopoulos (ed.) in *Alexander Hamilton's Pay Book* (Detroit: Wayne State University Press, 1961) that Hamilton had an additional source of English ideas, that of Malachy Postlethwayt's *The Universal Dictionary of Trade and Commerce*. As a young officer in 1776, Hamilton studied the Englishman's work and recorded numerous notes on his reading in the empty pages of the company's pay book.

It is quite possible that the careful perusal of this work, dated 1750, helped to temper Hamilton's enthusiasm for the rage of ideas on sinking funds that developed in the 1770's with the pamphleteering of Dr. Price. Reflecting the views of Englishmen who at the earlier date had become disillusioned in the efficacy of a sinking fund, Postlethwayt was very critical of not only a sinking fund but also of public debts, taxation, etc. Perhaps the ideas expressed in the *Dictionary* were still fresh enough in Hamilton's mind when he became Secretary of the Treasury that he did not accept uncritically the sinking fund ideas which were helping to maintain Pitt's popularity in England at the time.

The *Dictionary* also gave Hamilton the opportunity to become acquainted with the views of some of the authors with which Postlethwayt disagreed. The main point is that the careful reading of the *Dictionary* familiarized Hamilton with English thought on public finance and related subjects. He clearly was not influenced by the views of the author of the *Dictionary* to the extent of accepting Postlethwayt's position on public debts: Hamilton could still fervently argue that "a national debt, if it is not excessive, will be to us a national blessing."

5. ESTABLISHMENT OF HAMILTON'S FISCAL POLICIES: REPORTS, DEBATES, AND LAWS OF 1790

When the first Congress met in early 1789, the state of the public credit was extremely low and the market prices of the heterogeneous evidences of the public debt had depreciated to one-eighth their nominal value.[1] Because the Constitution had expressly stated that all debts previously contracted by the nation were valid against the United States, Congress had no choice but to seek some course of action to provide for the debt. As a preliminary measure, Congress enacted the temporary tariff of July 4, 1789, which was patterned after the federal import duties proposed by the Continental Congress.[2]

HAMILTON'S REPORT ON PUBLIC CREDIT

On September 21, 1789, the House of Representatives passed a resolution ordering the Secretary of the Treasury to prepare and submit to the House at its next session a plan for the adequate support of public credit.[3] This resolution had been made in accordance with the controversial provision in the act establishing the Treasury Department, which stated that "it shall be the duty of the Secretary of the Treasury to digest and prepare plans . . . for the support of public credit."[4] Regardless, the chain of events pertaining to the expected provision for the debt led to a state of public optimism, which by late 1789 revealed itself in a noticeable increase in the market price of public securities.[5]

Establishment of Public Credit. — Hamilton submitted his Report

1. Albert Gallatin, *The Writings of Albert Gallatin*, ed. Henry Adams (Philadelphia: J. B. Lippincott and Co., 1879), III, 127.
2. John Watts Kearny, *Sketch of American Finances 1789-1835* (New York: G. P. Putnam's Sons, 1887), p. 30.
3. U. S., *Annals of the Congress of the United States*, I, 904.
4. U. S., *Statutes at Large*, I, 65.
5. The barometer of public credit, according to the opinion of the time, was the market price of government debt: the nearer to par at which the debt sold, the higher was the public credit. A member of Congress was recorded as saying: "What is our object? To establish public credit — and that is found when the stock will sell at par" (*Annals of Congress*, II, 1441).

on the Public Credit to the House of Representatives on January 14, 1790. As Hamilton later explained in his Defense of the Funding System (date unknown), his Report on the Public Credit was based on the assumption that there were only three alternatives in selecting a plan for making provision for the debt.[6] One alternative was to pay off the principal and arrearages of interest immediately. This was, of course, impossible. A second alternative would be to provide annually for the interest on the debt and, as revenue permitted, to provide for the principal in the same manner. Leaving the debt in an unfunded state, however, would not enhance public credit to any great extent. The claims of the public creditors would be left to the mercy, partisanship, and intrigue of the House, Senate, or executive branches of government. New legislation each year would have to determine how much, if any, of the revenues were to be devoted to debt service. The remaining alternative, according to Hamilton, was to establish a funding system.

Determination of Size. — In his report of 1790, Hamilton proceeded first by determining the size of the national debt and its interest burden. He estimated the entire public debt (the debts of the United States and the individual states) at $79,124,465, including arrearages of interest.[7]

The debt of the United States amounted to $54,124,465. Of this total, the foreign debt accounted for $11,710,379: with $10,070,307 in principal and $1,640,072 in arrearages of interest to December 31, 1789. The rate of interest carried by the foreign debt was approximately 5 per cent. The domestic debt of the United States amounted to $42,414,086: that is $27,383,918 for principal; $13,030,168 for arrearages of interest to the end of 1790; and $2,000,000 in Continental bills of credit. The average rate of interest on the domestic debt was 6 per cent.

Hamilton estimated the state debts at $25,000,000, including both principal and arrearages of interest. The average rate of interest borne by the state debts was also 6 per cent.

Hamilton recommended making the entire public debt a debt of the national government. He justified the assumption of the state debts on the grounds that the state debts could be more adequately provided for by the national government and that the debts were contracted for the same purpose — "the price of liberty." The assumption of the state debts, according to Hamilton, would neither increase the total public debt of the nation nor increase the revenues required to service the public debt.

6. *Works of . . . Hamilton,* VIII, 430-36.
7. *American State Papers, Finance,* I, 19.

There was also the problem of how the national government was to handle the depreciated state of the domestic and state debts. A rather widespread opinion existed that a discrimination should be made between the original public creditors and the present holders of the debt by purchase. The latter group of creditors had obtained their claims against the government by purchasing the debt at a fraction of its nominal value. One solution proposed was to make full provision for the debt of a public creditor only if he were the original holder of the debt. The public creditors by purchase would be provided for only in accordance with the depreciated price at which they purchased the debt. Hamilton's position, however, was that a policy of discrimination would be unjust and ruinous to the establishment of public credit. It would be a breach of contract, and contrary to the provision in the Constitution that expressly pledged the public faith of the new government to provide for the debts of the old government.

Conversion to a Lower Rate of Interest. — Hamilton was now prepared to consider the question of whether the entire public debt of $79,124,465 could be funded.[8] Computing an interest charge on the principal of the domestic and state debts at 6 per cent, the foreign debt at 5 per cent, and the arrearages of interest at 4 per cent, the annual amount of interest payable on the total debt would be $4,587,445. The question reduced itself to whether the revenues of the United States could be increased sufficiently to meet an annual funding bill of $4,587,-445, in addition to the sum necessary for the current service of the government.

Hamilton believed that the funding of the debt in its present form would require too great an extension of taxation. Before funding could take place, therefore, the existing rate of interest on the domestic and state components of the public debt, which averaged 6 per cent, had to be reduced. Hamilton emphasized that the foreign debt should be funded according to the precise terms of the contracts with the foreign creditors.

A reduction in the rate of interest on the debt would be possible, according to Hamilton, if the government offered the public creditors a fair equivalent in exchange for a voluntary modification of their interest claims. Since it was a matter of the government's discretion when to pay the principal, the government could take advantage of a future fall in the market rate of interest by paying off the public creditors and converting the debt to a lower rate of interest by a new loan. The redeemable quality of the debt, therefore, was favorable to the govern-

8. *Ibid.*

ment, but unfavorable to the public creditors. The equivalent, therefore, that Hamilton proposed to give the public creditors in exchange for a modification of their interest claims was a limitation on the redeemable quality of the debt.

To accomplish the conversion of the debt to a lower rate of interest, Hamilton proposed that a loan, to the full amount of the domestic and state debts, be contracted on an exchange basis. In exchange for their existing holdings of 6 per cent redeemable debt, including arrearages of interest, the public creditors would have their choice of securities which compensated for the reduction of interest, either by a limit placed on the amount which could be redeemed in one year, or, as an auxiliary equivalent, by payments in western lands. Hamilton also suggested that another security, a tontine, be offered to the public creditors. These new securities would have the effect of reducing the interest on the debt to 4 per cent.[9]

Hamilton's reason for offering several types of securities was to make the exchange loan attractive to enough public creditors to assure the conversion of the debt to a lower rate of interest, for poor public response would not lower the average rate of interest on the debt sufficiently to make a funding system fulfill its purpose:

> Arrears of interest, continually accruing, will be as continual a monument, either of inability or of ill faith, and will not cease to have an evil influence on public credit. In nothing are appearances of greater moment than whatever regards credit. Opinion is the soul of it; and this is affected by appearances as well as realities.[10]

The Funding System. — Hamilton was now prepared to make his funding proposal. It was to be the new debt created by the loan, in addition to the foreign debt, that was to be funded, not the domestic and state debts in their old form.

Hamilton calculated that the present duties on imports and tonnage, which were the only sources of the national revenue (other than the post office), did not produce sufficient revenue at their present rates to provide for both the interest on the debt and the current service of government. Hamilton proposed a plan calling for increased duties on wines, spirits, teas, and coffee, which would make the revenues adequate for the funding operation. The revenue from the combined duties should then be pledged to the payment of interest on the foreign debt and the new loan "by an appropriation coextensive with the duration of the debt."[11]

9. *Ibid.,* I, 20-21.   10. *Ibid.,* I, 22.   11. *Ibid.,* I, 24.

The Sinking Fund. — Hamilton pointed out that the revenues from the duties on imports and tonnage had been mortgaged to the public creditors, but that the revenues from the post office had been left untouched. This source of revenue, Hamilton continued, should be appropriated to a sinking fund.[12]

The net revenue of the post office, according to Hamilton's plan, would be vested in commissioners, to consist of the President of the Senate, the Speaker of the House of Representatives, the Chief Justice, the Secretary of the Treasury, and the Attorney-General, to be used for the discharge of debt, either by purchases of stock in the market or by payments on the amount yearly redeemable on the principal of the new stock, until the whole debt was discharged. Hamilton also proposed that the commissioners be authorized to borrow sums not to exceed $12,000,-000, for the purpose either of converting the foreign debt to a lower rate of interest, or of purchasing domestic debt in the market when it was selling below par.

DEBATES, REPORTS, AND LAWS OF 1790

Debates in Congress. — Hamilton's report was read in the House of Representatives on January 14, 1790. Earnest debate on Hamilton's report did not begin until February 8, when Thomas Fitzsimmons of Pennsylvania proposed the following resolution:

> *Resolved*, That permanent funds ought to be appropriated for the payment of interest on, and the gradual discharge of, the domestic debt of the United States.[13]

The permanent appropriation of funds was the essential ingredient to a funding system or a sinking fund. The resolution immediately produced some debate in Congress.

Objections to the funding proposal centered around the fear that the permanent appropriation of revenues would create a perpetual debt like that of England's.[14] Representative Smith of South Carolina, however, emphasized that the resolution called for the establishment of a sinking fund.[15] A sinking fund, he argued, should ease the minds of those who feared a permanent debt. Those who opposed the establishment of a sinking fund cited Adam Smith as an authority.[16]

12. *Ibid.*
14. *Ibid.*, I, 1140-64.
16. *Ibid.*, I, 1144; II, 1174.

13. *Annals of Congress*, I, 1138.
15. *Ibid.*, I, 1144.

On February 22, Fitzsimmons' resolution was approved, and the debates in Congress became completely absorbed in the highly controversial policies of discrimination and assumption. As Fisher Ames said to the House of Representatives at a later date, almost no opposition to Hamilton's funding system was expressed in the first Congress.[17] The funding plan was adopted by a large majority and was supported by public opinion. The opposition to Hamilton's plan was confined almost entirely to his proposals for assuming the state debts and for making no discrimination between types of public creditors.

Hamilton's Report of August 7, 1790. — Congress decided that the funding system would not commence until the first day of January, 1791. Hamilton saw that there would be a surplus above current service of over $1,000,000 from the duties in operation to the end of the year, and he wrote a report to the House of Representatives suggesting that it would be expedient to apply the surplus to the purchase of debt in the market.[18] The purchases would be made through the sinking fund. Since the public stock was still selling well below par, the employing of the surplus and proceeds of loans in the purchase of debt would make a sizable reduction in the principal of the debt. The amount of debt reduction obtained by this expedient would depend, of course, upon the timing of the purchases. At a later date, the expected rise in the price of the government stocks would not permit the surplus to retire as much debt as it would now.

Funding and Sinking Fund Legislation. — Hamilton's proposals for the establishment of public credit were enacted into law by three acts passed by Congress in August of 1790.

The act of August 4, 1790, entitled "An Act making provision for the Debt of the United States,"[19] commonly called the Funding Act, provided for the assumption of the state debts, adjusted to $21,500,000, and authorized a loan, subscribable in old debt, to the full amount of the domestic and assumed state debts. The loan would convert the debt into 6 per cent, 6 per cent deferred, and 3 per cent stocks. The 6 per cent and 3 per cent stocks would begin to bear interest on January 1, 1791, and the 6 per cent deferred stock would begin to bear interest on January 1, 1801. For each subscription in the principal of the domestic debt, two-thirds of the principal would be converted into 6 per cent stock and one-third into 6 per cent deferred stock. Arrearages of inter-

17. January 16, 1795, *Ibid.,* IV, 1106.
18. August 7, 1791, *American State Papers, Finance,* I, 63.
19. *Statutes at Large,* I, 138-44.

52

est on the domestic debt would be exchanged for 3 per cent stock. For each subscription in the principal and arrearages of interest of the state debts, four-ninths of the principal would be converted into 6 per cent stock, two-ninths into 6 per cent deferred stock, and one-third into 3 per cent stock.

The 6 per cent stock would be subject to redemption by payments not exceeding, in one year, on account of both principal and interest, eight dollars on every hundred of the original sum subscribed. The 6 per cent deferred stock was not redeemable until 1801, at which time it would be subject to the same rate of redemption as the 6 per cent stock. The 3 per cent stock was redeemable without limit.

The act then provided for the funding of the debt by inviolably pledging the duties on imports and tonnage to the payment of interest on the foreign, domestic, and state debts, in that order, until the final redemption of the whole debt. It also authorized the President to borrow up to $12,000,000 to service the arrearages of interest and principal on the foreign debt. Finally, the act pledged the proceeds of the sales of western lands to the discharge of debt.

The act of August 10, 1790, entitled "An Act making further provision for the payment of the debts of the United States,"[20] supplemented the funding act by providing for an increase in the duties on certain imported articles.

The act of August 12, 1790, entitled "An Act making provision for the reduction of the Public Debt,"[21] appropriated the surplus duties on imports and tonnage to the end of the year 1790 for the purchase of debt. All purchases were to be made by the commissioners (the high officers of state suggested by Hamilton). The President was authorized to borrow up to $2,000,000, at an interest rate not exceeding 5 per cent, for the purchase of debt.

Hamilton's Report on a National Bank. — A funding system and a sinking fund having been established, the House of Representatives ordered Hamilton "to prepare and report . . . such further provision as may . . . be necessary for establishing the public credit."[22] On December 14, 1790, Hamilton responded by submitting his famous Report on a National Bank.

Hamilton's discussion of the need for a national bank still rested primarily on his beliefs that there was "a deficiency of circulating

20. *Ibid.*, I, 180-82.
21. *Ibid.*, I, 186-87.
22. *Annals of Congress*, II, 1723.

medium," that national banks encouraged trade and industry, and that national banks were of benefit to the government.[23]

Hamilton's plan called for a national bank under private direction,[24] with capital stock not to exceed $10,000,000. Subscriptions by the public were to total $8,000,000, and were to be payable one-fourth in specie and three-fourths in that portion of the funded debt of the United States bearing a present rate of interest of 6 per cent. The United States was to subscribe to the remaining $2,000,000 of the bank's stock.

One purpose in using the funded debt in the formation of the bank's capital, Hamilton explained, was "the creation of a capital sufficiently large to be the basis of an extensive circulation, and an adequate security for it."[25] Since it was impossible to collect $10,000,000 in specie, an auxiliary capital was needed. Hamilton pointed out that the fitness of public debt as the basis of a paper circulation was illustrated by the example of the Bank of England.[26]

Hamilton had another purpose in mind in using the funded debt in the formation of the bank's capital. The requirement that three-fourths of the public's subscriptions be paid in debt would create a demand for $6,000,000 of funded debt. The formation of the bank would contribute greatly to raising the market price of government stock to par, which would benefit the public creditors and help in the quick establishment of public credit.

The subscription of $2,000,000 by the United States was, according to Hamilton, for the purpose of enlarging the specie fund of the bank. However, since the government did not have $2,000,000 in specie to spare at the time, an expedient would have to be substituted. The government would purchase the stock by means of a loan from the bank.

23. *American State Papers, Finance*, I, 67-71. Bolles has agreed with Hamilton's analysis of the need for a national bank. The total capital of the three banks in America amounted to only $2,000,000. Barter conditions were still prevalent in some places, and there was a meager supply of coin. See Albert S. Bolles, *The Financial History of the United States from 1789 to 1860* (New York: D. Appleton and Company, 1885), p. 127.

24. Hamilton considered making the bank under public direction, but decided that it might be subject to abuse in a national emergency. Full public confidence in the bank and its paper circulation was dependent, Hamilton concluded, on its being under private direction.

25. *American State Papers, Finance*, I, 75.

26. It may be noted that, contrary to the implicit assumption of some writers, Hamilton did not refrain from citing an English precedent, if one existed, for his proposals.

The loan would be reimbursable in ten equal yearly installments. The annual reimbursements in specie, therefore, would accomplish the investment of specie needed by the bank.

On February 25, 1791, a national bank was created by the act entitled "An Act to incorporate the subscribers to the Bank of the United States."[27] The corporation was granted a charter to March 4, 1811. The act made no significant changes in Hamilton's proposals.

27. *Statutes at Large,* I, 191-96.

6. HAMILTON'S FISCAL POLICIES IN OPERATION: 1791-1795

T he impact on public credit which Hamilton expected from his fiscal policies was not long in forthcoming. The terms of the conversion loan were widely accepted by the public creditors, with the effect of reducing the rate of interest on the whole debt, foreign, domestic, and assumed, to an average of about $4\frac{1}{2}$ per cent.[1] The funding of the debt, the purchases of debt by the sinking fund, and the large demand for funded debt in the payment of bank subscriptions had a favorable effect on the price of government debt. By July of 1791, the market price of the 6 per cent funded stock was at par.[2] By March of 1792, the 6 per cent stock was selling at a 25 per cent premium.[3] Hamilton's policies also resulted in altering the terms on which America borrowed abroad. Within a year the United States had changed from a nation with weak credit to one that could borrow on the same terms as the leading nations of Europe.[4]

Operation of the Funding System, 1791-1795

The domestic and assumed components of the American funding system were not expanded during Hamilton's administration. The difference between the size of the funded domestic debt on January 1, 1791, and January 1, 1795 (see Table 1)[5], was a result of the gradual

1. Hamilton to Washington, August 18, 1792, *Works of . . . Hamilton*, II, 443.
2. *American State Papers, Finance*, I, 231.
3. For graphic presentations of the fluctuations in the prices of the various funded securities through 1792, see Davis, pp. 187, 210.
4. Kearny, p. 8.
5. It is difficult to obtain an exact picture of the size of the various debt components for each of the years between 1790 and 1797. There were no yearly statements of the national debt made by the Treasury Department during these years. Actually, certain components of the funding system did not become funded on January 1, 1791, but were spaced out during this period; for example, the settlement of accounts between debtor and creditor states. Usually, however, these components are treated as if they were funded on January 1, 1791. When yearly figures for the period 1791-1795 are given without treating certain items as funded at the beginning of the period, then it produces the appearance that the funding system was expanded by almost $5,000,000 during Hamilton's administration. See U.S., Treasury Department, *Annual Report of the Secretary of the Treasury on the State of the Finances* (1896) p. xciii.

TABLE 1

Operation of the Funding System Under Hamilton's Administration

PRE-FUNDING DEBT COMPONENTS	UNFUNDED DEBT Jan. 9, 1790[a]	DEBT COMPONENTS AFTER ESTABLISHMENT OF FUNDING SYSTEM	FUNDED AND UNFUNDED DEBT Jan. 1, 1791[b]	FUNDED AND UNFUNDED DEBT Jan. 1, 1795[c]
Foreign debt	$11,710,379	Funded foreign debt	$12,513,341	$13,745,379
Domestic debt	42,414,086	Funded domestic debt	44,448,759[d]	44,783,123[d]
State debts	25,000,000	Funded state debts	18,271,815	18,271,815
Total debt	$79,124,465	Total funded debt	$75,233,915	$76,800,317
		Purchases of the sinking fund	278,687	2,265,023
		Total net funded debt	$74,955,228	$74,535,294
		Unsubscribed debt	2,127,514	1,561,175
		Anticipations (bank loans)		2,900,000[e]
		Total net funded and unfunded debt	$77,082,742	$78,996,469[f]

[a] *American State Papers, Finance*, I, 19.

[b] *Ibid.*, I, 484.

[c] *Ibid.*, I, 325-26, 339.

[d] Includes balances owed to creditor states of $4,221,101.

[e] *American State Papers, Finance*, I, 372, 661-63; and Rafael A. Bayley, *The National Loans of the United States from July 4, 1776, to June 30, 1880*, pp. 28-30, 35-38, 108, and 112-15.

[f] Omitted from the table is the $1,400,000 balance owed to the Bank of the United States for the $2,000,000 subscription loan.

acceptance of the terms of the conversion loan by a minority of public creditors holding unsubscribed debt.[6] In fact, there was a net reduction in the domestic and assumed components of the funded debt during Hamilton's administration, as the sinking fund purchased $2,265,023 worth of debt (see Table 2).

TABLE 2

OPERATION OF THE SINKING FUND UNDER HAMILTON'S ADMINISTRATION

	INCOME OF SINKING FUND				DEBT PURCHASED
YEAR	from Surplus Revenue	from Foreign Loans	from Interest[a]	Total	
1790	$150,239			$ 150,239	$ 278,687
1791	549,683		$ 6	549,689	852,677
1792	257,786		25,970	283,756	379,165
1793		$334,902	76,843	411,745	508,665
1794	67	100,000	85,833	185,900	245,828
Total	$957,775	$434,902	$188,652	$1,581,329	$2,265,022

Source: American State Papers, Finance, I, 81-82, 111-22, 162-71, 302-16, and 234-48. Also, Gallatin, *The Writings of Albert Gallatin,* p. 197.

[a]This source of income included both the interest on the debt purchased and the interest on debt paid into the treasury in satisfaction of debt owed to the United States. Debt redeemed in the latter manner amounted to $395,820.

That the funding system was not used as a system of domestic borrowing does not mean, of course, that no new borrowing of any kind took place during the period in question. On several occasions Hamilton found the revenues insufficient to cover expenditures. The Indian wars, the strained relations with England, the Algerine troubles, and the western insurrection all produced unusual expenses. For these exigencies, duties on imports were increased in 1792 and 1794, and duties were levied on carriages, retail wine and foreign liquor sales, snuff, sugar, and property sold at auction. Since the purposes for which these duties were levied could not wait upon the receipt of the revenues, the new revenues had to be anticipated to meet the unexpected and urgent occasions of new expense. During Hamilton's administration, therefore, temporary loans in anticipation of revenue were obtained from the Bank of New York on three occasions, the Bank of North America on two occasions, and the Bank of the United States on four occasions. On

6. The deadline for subscribing to the conversion loan was extended on several occasions. The loan was finally closed on December 31, 1797.

January 1, 1795, the balance owed on these loans was $2,900,000. It is quite unlikely that Hamilton contemplated reproducing the English practice of building up a large floating debt, funding it, and then repeating the same process over again, because the temporary loans were genuine anticipations in the sense that the new revenues were adequate to liquidate their respective loans.

The foreign component of the American funding system grew slightly (see Table 1), but not because it was a funding system of the English variety. If Hamilton had desired to use a funding system to finance government and to erect a perpetual debt, it is doubtful that he would have expanded the foreign debt for those purposes, for he clearly saw the difference between an internally held and an externally held debt.[7] During Hamilton's administration, eight loans totaling $9,400,000 were contracted in Holland to meet the charges on the original foreign debts. The proceeds of the loans are accounted for by the retirement of the original foreign debt, by $600,000, allocated to the payment of the subscription debt to the bank, by $450,395 for the discharge of miscellaneous claims against the government, and by $434,902 for sinking fund purchases of domestic debt.

OPERATION OF THE SINKING FUND, 1791-1795

By English standards, the sinking fund established in America in 1790 was a mechanism of little value. It had no permanent appropriation out of the general revenues to serve as a basis for the accumulative powers of a sum expanding by compound interest. Congress had given the sinking fund only limited sources of income, the surplus revenues of 1790 and the proceeds of foreign loans not exceeding $2,000,000. The surplus revenue used to purchase debt in 1790 amounted to $150,239; with this sum, debt having a par value of $278,687 was purchased.[8] Purchases of debt below par continued to be made in the succeeding years. The total amount expended for this purpose by the end of 1794 amounted to $1,392,677: $957,775 from the surplus revenues of 1790, and $434,902 from the proceeds of foreign loans. The debt purchased by these two latter sums had a combined par value of $1,994,804. Obviously, no great inroads on the national debt could be made with just these sources of income.

But the American sinking fund was more successful than it might

7. *Works of . . . Hamilton*, VIII, 453-54.
8. *American State Papers, Finance*, I, 81-82.

at first appear. The explanation is that Hamilton had other purposes in mind when proposing the sinking fund of 1790. Congress was almost unanimous in wanting some provision made for the principal of the debt. Hamilton's political foes, including Jefferson and Madison, had approached Hamilton and urged that the debt be placed in the process of extinguishment. In fact, Jefferson, who was always ready to accuse Hamilton of being a copyist of English ideas, probably wanted Hamilton to set up a sinking fund of the kind advocated by Dr. Price.[9] There was also the pressure for the establishment of a sinking fund from influential businessmen like William Bingham and Stephen Higginson.[10] Hamilton, who was a practicing political analyst as well as a financier, could not overlook these varied sources of pressure. Among other reasons, therefore, he had a political purpose in mind in establishing and operating the poorly-endowed sinking fund of 1790. Although Hamilton was never able to satisfy the Jeffersonian faction, either with the sinking fund or any other policy, he was successful in satisfying most of the other political and economic interests with which he had to contend.

Related to the foregoing purpose was another objective of Hamilton's sinking fund, that of enhancing the public credit by psychological means. Hamilton was thoroughly convinced that in things pertaining to public credit, nothing counted quite so much as "sounds and appearances." "Appearances," he said, were as important as "realities." Hamilton gave the public precisely those appearances for which they were looking. He proposed that the highest officers in the government, as in England, be denominated as commissioners and be charged with the management of a sinking fund. Hamilton, as one of his contemporary critics has pointed out, was interested in forms and apparatus.[11] The existence of the sinking fund machinery gave the appearance that

9. After all the accusations made by Jefferson and his associates concerning Hamilton's desire to copy the English system of finance, it is strange to find that Jefferson once wrote: "Dr. Price, in his book on annuities, has given a valuable chapter on the effects of a sinking fund" (Jefferson to John W. Eppes, September 11, 1813, *The Writings of . . . Jefferson* [ed. Lipscomb], XIII, 367). This was written *after* the contradictory and costly effects of Dr. Price's ideas had become fairly well known. Jefferson, in this single statement, gave more recognition to Dr. Price and the compound-interest principle than Hamilton did in all of his reports, letters, and other writings combined.

10. Higginson to Hamilton, November, 1789, Wettereau, pp. 683-86.

11. Gallatin in Henry Adams, *The Life of Albert Gallatin* (Philadelphia: J. B. Lippincott and Company, 1879), p. 296.

the debt was being paid[12] and that all the ingredients of a well-constructed fiscal system had been furnished.

Hamilton used every possible opportunity to obtain the full psychological and political value out of what little debt redemption the sinking fund accomplished. For instance, in 1792, after the sinking fund had purchased $1,456,743 of debt with $941,851 of specie, Hamilton had a circular printed on the sinking fund's activities and sent to all the newspapers. He enclosed a statement requesting that the editors "give the information the general circulation which its importance merits."[13] Except for the readers of anti-Federalist newspapers like the National Gazette, this information no doubt made an impression on the minds of the public.[14]

OPERATION OF THE BANK OF THE UNITED STATES, 1791-1795

On December 12, 1791, the Bank of the United States opened for business. Thomas Willing, a former business partner of Robert Morris and the first president of the Bank of North America, was selected president of the new national bank.

Other than the creation of a $6,000,000 demand for government 6 per cent stock, the Bank of the United States had no relationship to the American funding system. All government loans contracted from the bank during Hamilton's administration were temporary loans. While the revenue system was being expanded, Hamilton frequently had to anticipate newly-levied revenues to meet expenses coming due. Hamilton found that the Bank of the United States and, to a lesser extent, the Bank of New York and the Bank of North America were useful for this purpose. Hamilton had no thought of financing the government by the incorporation of debt in a national bank, nor in any other institution. The Bank of the United States, therefore, never assumed a role in America comparable to the Bank of England's role in English fiscal arrangements.

12. This motive of Hamilton's is probably the key to Jefferson's criticism. Jefferson, in a letter to Albert Gallatin, the Secretary of the Treasury between 1801 and 1813, wrote at length on the point that Hamilton's policies were designed merely to give the impression that the debt was being paid. Apparently Jefferson jumped to the conclusion that Hamilton didn't want the debt paid (Jefferson to Gallatin, April 1, 1802, *The Writings of ... Jefferson* [ed. Lipscomb], X, 306-9).

13. *Works of ... Hamilton*, III, 24.

14. Philip Freneau, the editor of the *National Gazette*, published Hamilton's circular, but accompanied it with an editorial which charged that the national debt had increased since the funding system had been established (*ibid.*, III, 28).

The Bank of the United States was highly successful in fulfilling its economic functions. According to a recent historian and enthusiastic admirer of the bank, it became the "mainspring and regulator of the whole American business world."[15] Its customers were mainly whole-sale merchants, manufacturers, master mechanics, and wealthy land-owners. It no doubt made a significant contribution to the development of the economy.

ALTERATION, OPERATION, AND CRITICISM
OF THE SINKING FUND, 1792-1794

The remaining history of Hamilton's fiscal policies centered around the sinking fund. No innovations were made in the funding system or national bank after their establishment. The sinking fund, however, became the subject of several reports and additional legislation.

Systematic Sinking Fund of 1792. — On November 1, 1791, the House of Representatives passed a resolution requesting the Secretary of the Treasury to suggest measures that would complete the objects of the funding and sinking fund laws of 1790.[16] Hamilton responded with his report of February 7, 1792.

In his report, Hamilton reviewed the intention of Congress in 1790 to extinguish the debt as fast as possible, and then submitted the following "systematic plan" for augmenting the effectiveness of the sinking fund:

> An obvious basis of this establishment . . . is the amount of interest on as much of the debt as has been, or shall be, from time to time, purchased, or paid off, or received in discharge of any debt or demand of the United States, . . . over and above the interest of any new debt, which may be created, in order to such purchase or payment.
>
> It is therefore submitted, that it be adopted as a principle, that all the interest which shall have ceased to be payable by any of the means above specified, shall be set apart and appropriated, in the most firm and inviolable manner as a fund for sinking the public debt, by purchase or payment. . . .[17]

Hamilton's proposal for a systematic sinking fund produced no debates in Congress, and the plan was quickly enacted into law. The act

15. James O. Wettereau, "New Light on the First Bank of the United States," *Pennsylvania Magazine of History and Biography*, LXI (1937), 263.
16. *Annals of Congress*, III, 150.
17. *American State Papers, Finance*, I, 148.

of May 8, 1792, entitled "An Act supplementary to the Act making provision for the Debt of the United States,"[18] inviolably pledged two new sources of income to the sinking fund: (1) the interest on the debt purchased, redeemed, or otherwise acquired by the sinking fund, and (2) the surplus, if any, of the revenues appropriated for the payment of interest on the public debt.

Resemblance to the English Model. — The act of 1792 gave the sinking fund its first permanent source of income, the interest on debt purchased, redeemed, or otherwise acquired by the sinking fund. Neither of the two original sources of income—the surplus revenue of the year 1790 and the borrowing authority of $2,000,000—could be classified as a permanent source of income.

It has been said that the permanent income feature in the new sinking fund legislation produced a sinking fund similar to Pitt's.[19] It will be seen, however, that the sinking fund of 1792 was essentially still the feeble purchase fund of 1790, not a powerful sinking fund of the English variety.

Actually, the amount of the permanent income inviolably appropriated to the purchase of debt by the act of 1792 was rather insignificant. The debt held by the sinking fund commissioners on January 1, 1792, totaled $1,131,365: $311,123 in 6 per cent stock; $309,622 in 3 per cent stock; and $510,620 in deferred 6 per cent stock. The interest from a holding of debt of that size and variety would have given the sinking fund an income in one year of only $27,956. The growth of the permanent source of the sinking fund's income, which was the interest on the debt held, was bound to be slow. The growth that it registered (see Table 1) was largely due to the additional interest income received from $395,820 worth of government stock paid into the Treasury in satisfaction of debts owed to the United States. The total interest income from all sources obtained by the sinking fund during Hamilton's administration amounted to only $188,652. With this sum, the sinking fund purchased debt with a par value of $270,219.

For the purpose of debt extinguishment, the provision for appropriating the interest on the debt held was only a token income. In order to be a reproduction of Pitt's, what Hamilton's sinking fund really needed was a permanent appropriation of an absolute amount out of the general revenues. Instead, only a contingent source of income was

18. *Statutes at Large,* I, 281-83.
19. Ross, pp. 41-42.

added to the interest income of the sinking fund — the surplus of revenues appropriated for the payment of interest on the public debt. This provision tied the growth of the sinking fund to the growth of the revenue system. Until the anticipated growth materialized, the sinking fund's purpose had to be confined largely to its support policy, not to the extinguishment of debt.

The conclusion that the act of 1792 established a sinking fund based on the principles that produced the English financial fiasco is also unwarranted from an examination of the writings of Hamilton. Nowhere in any of Hamilton's reports, letters, or other writings can be found an analysis of a sinking fund that was even remotely similar to the type of analysis that was common to the English writers. The English and the Hamiltonian sinking funds were based on different theoretical foundations. Hamilton was not "half mad" over the "magic" of a sinking fund. He did not believe that a large national debt could be paid off at a small expense, or that the commissioners of the sinking fund could borrow at simple interest to pay off debt at compound interest. The magical power of compound interest was not the principle which Hamilton had in mind in proposing the sinking fund of 1792. He could, of course, have paid nominal homage to the compound-interest principle by mentioning it in some of his arguments for the support of his proposals. Instead, he completely ignored the great discovery of Dr. Price.

It would appear that Hamilton's advocacy of the "systematic plan" was based on a belief that the benefits to be derived from the provision compensated for the risk involved. The public would be favorably impressed by a plan of debt redemption based on an inviolable appropriation of the interest income of the sinking fund to the purchase or redemption of debt. The potentially dangerous provision, which meant that in the year 1792 less than $30,000 would be inviolably appropriated to the purchase of debt, was no doubt infinitely more effective in serving the Federalist party and other political ends, and in satisfying the moneyed interests, than the same sum would have been if obtained and allocated to the purchase of debt in any other way.

Criticism of Hamilton's Fiscal Policies. — The sinking fund legislation of 1792 did not satisfy the more dedicated and impassioned critics of Hamilton's administration. The attacks of the Jeffersonian faction only seemed to increase. The *National Gazette* began to run editorials accusing Hamilton of believing that public debts were public blessings. The attack had even reached the point of influencing President Washington. During a trip to Virginia, Washington heard so many objections to Hamilton's policies that he was compelled to write Hamilton for an explanation. Washington's letter of July 29, 1792, listed twenty-one objections to Hamilton's fiscal program.

The Virginia critics had resurrected the controversies over the assumption of the state debts and over the discrimination between original and present holders of the debt. They now also attacked the principle of funding, which had not been a topic of serious controversy in the first Congress. Their new argument was that the funding system had not only created debt, but that it also had perpetuated debt. The critics had even linked Hamilton's fiscal policies to what they believed was Hamilton's aim to establish a monarchy in the United States.

The objection which was made in the strongest terms was that which accused Hamilton of not desiring to see the debt paid off. In evidence of this charge, the critics had pointed out the limited redemption feature of the 6 per cent stocks. Hamilton's defense, of course, was that the limited right of redemption reserved to the government was necessary to effect a voluntary reduction in the rate of interest borne by the debt, and that a greater right would have been beyond the nation's ability to redeem debt.[20]

One of the Virginians who remained unsatisfied by the sinking fund legislation of 1792 was Thomas Jefferson. On September 9, 1792, Jefferson could still write the following to President Washington:

> No man is more ardently intent to see the public debt soon and sacredly paid off than I am. This exactly marks the difference between . . . Hamilton's views and mine, that I would wish the debt paid tomorrow; he wishes it never to be paid, but always to be a thing wherewith to corrupt and manage the Legislature.[21]

When Jefferson stated that he wanted the debt paid off "tomorrow," he meant almost that, since he believed it was contrary to the "laws of nature" not to provide for the payment of an existing public debt in a period of nineteen years or less.[22] If the period of payment extended any longer, the succeeding generation would have to pay the debts of the present generation.

Hamilton's Redemption Plan of 1792. — The movement for making a more effective provision for the discharge of the national debt began

20. Hamilton to Washington, August 18, 1792, *Works of . . . Hamilton,* II, 445.
21. *The Writings of . . . Jefferson* (ed. Lipscomb), VIII, 401.
22. Jefferson to John W. Eppes, June 24, 1813, *ibid.,* XIII, 270-73.

to take the form of demanding that the government exercise its right to redeem the 6 per cent stock. On November 6, 1792, Washington addressed a joint meeting of both houses of Congress in these words:

> I entertain a strong hope that the state of our national finances is now sufficiently matured to enable you to enter upon a systematic and effectual arrangement for the regular redemption and discharge of the Public Debt, according to the right which has been reserved to the Government; no measure can be more desirable, whether viewed with an eye to its intrinsic importance, or to the general sentiment and wish of the nation.[23]

The House of Representatives answered the President's message by passing a resolution directing Hamilton to report a plan for "the redemption of so much of the public debt as the . . . United States have reserved the right to redeem."[24]

In his report of December 3, 1792, Hamilton pointed out that the expense of conducting the Indian wars had made the existing revenues inadequate for debt redemption.[25] If Congress, Hamilton continued, did not wish to wait until peace returned, at which time a surplus would appear, then the levying of additional revenues would be unavoidable. Hamilton suggested that the most effective and economical plan would be to levy new taxes equal to sums annually redeemable. After pointing out the magnitude to which the revenues of the United States had grown in three years, Hamilton suggested that an additional sudden and sizable tax levy might have unwanted repercussions.

Hamilton believed that, under the existing circumstances, the best plan would be to borrow amounts equal to the sums annually redeemable, and to levy taxes to form an income sufficient not only to pay the interest but to extinguish the principal on the new loan by January 1, 1802. This plan would accomplish (1) the complete discharge of the debt annually redeemable and (2) the complete reimbursement, in the same period, of all auxiliary loans. Hamilton's plan called for new taxes of only $43,199 in the first year of its operation. But new taxes would be levied each year for seven years, at the end of which time the yearly revenue from the new taxes would be $691,649. The beauty of Hamilton's plan was that the government could immediately exercise its full right of debt redemption while imposing new taxes in a gradual man-

23. *Annals of Congress*, III, 610.
24. *Ibid.*, III, 711, 722.
25. *American State Papers, Finance*, I, 176.

ner. Nevertheless, Hamilton's plan never met the approval of Congress.[26]

Improved Position of the Revenues in 1795. — The year 1794 was full of financial embarrassments for the United States. Because of the strained relations with England and the interruptions to foreign commerce, appropriations had increased and revenues had fallen off so that several new taxes had to be established during the year. By November of 1794, however, foreign relations had improved. The prospects were bright for a sizable surplus of revenue over expenditures for the year 1795. The movement to make a more effective provision for redeeming the debt had been somewhat dormant since 1793, but it was now resumed in full force.

The President's speech to Congress on November 19, 1794, expressed the growing demand for a permanent appropriation of revenue to the redemption of debt. Washington said:

> The time which has elapsed since the commencement of our financial measures has developed our pecuniary resources, so as to open the way for a definitive plan for the redemption of the Public Debt. . . . Nothing can more promote the permanent welfare of the nation, and nothing would be more grateful to our constituents. Indeed, whatsoever is unfinished of our system of public credit, cannot be benefited by procrastination; and, as far as may be practicable, we ought to place that credit on grounds which cannot be disturbed.[27]

Two days later the House of Representatives reacted to Washington's message by ordering a committee of the House to report a plan for providing for the payment of the debt. The instructions were for a plan "not temporary or annual, but systematic and permanent."[28]

HAMILTON'S VALEDICTORY REPORT

The House of Representatives had not ordered the Secretary of the Treasury to prepare the plan. The constitutionality of such a procedure had become a subject of heated debate. By this time, however, Hamilton was contemplating resigning his office, and on December 1, 1794, he officially announced his intention to resign on January 31, 1795.[29] Hamilton also decided to prepare a plan for debt redemption on his own initiative.

26. The debates in Congress show that there was an opposition to levying new taxes at this time (*Annals of Congress*, III, 870-73).

27. *Ibid.*, IV, 791-92. 28. *Ibid.*, IV, 1016.

29. Hamilton to Speaker of the House of Representatives, *Works of . . . Hamilton*, III, 199.

Extinguishment Plan. — The plan that Hamilton submitted to both houses of Congress called for paying off the entire national debt, foreign and domestic, funded and unfunded, in a period not exceeding thirty years.[30] Hamilton calculated the sums required to secure firmly the redemption of the present and deferred 6 per cent stocks, according to the right reserved by the government in the funding act. Since the principal redeemable the first year on the 6 per cent stocks was limited to 2 per cent of the total outstanding, then the sum redeemable on the present 6 per cent stocks, exclusive of the amount held by the creditor states and the sinking fund, was $516,410; the corresponding sum redeemable on the deferred 6 per cent stocks after 1802 was $249,577.[31] Hamilton's immediate problem, therefore, was to secure an income for the sinking fund which, in addition to its existing income, would secure the redemption of these two components of the national debt.

In order to redeem the 6 per cent stock, the sinking fund would need $408,134, in addition to its present income of $106,364.[32] The necessary $516,410 would then be secured. In order to redeem the 6 per cent deferred stock by annual payments after 1802 of $249,576, the sinking fund would need an additional income of only $44,756, because by that time the sinking fund would have an additional interest income of $52,319 from its holdings of deferred 6 per cent stock, and an additional income from bank stock dividends of $152,500. The total annual appropriation needed to secure the redemption of the stocks in question, therefore, would be $408,134 until 1802, and afterwards would be $452,891.

The complete redemption of the present 6 per cent and deferred 6 per cent stocks in 1818 and 1824, respectively, would set the revenues allocated for interest and redemption payments free for the redemption and purchase of the remainder of the debt. The sums released by the redemption of the present 6 per cent stock would discharge the foreign debt in six years. The sums released by the redemption of the deferred 6 per cent stock would, with the help of the sum released by the payment of the foreign debt, redeem the stock held by the creditor states and the unfunded debt in two years. The 3 per cent stock would be redeemed by the proceeds of the sales of western lands by 1826, at which time the entire debt would be extinguished.

In order to constitute a sinking fund sufficient to extinguish the

30. *American State Papers, Finance,* I, 326-31.
31. *Ibid.,* I, 326.   32. *Ibid.,* I, 344.

national debt in a period of thirty years or less, Hamilton proposed that the sinking fund's income be augmented by the following appropriations: (1) so much of the revenue from the permanent duties as, together with its existing income, would be sufficient for the sinking fund, in 1796 and thereafter, to redeem yearly the present 6 per cent stock; (2) so much of the permanent duties as, together with the dividends on the stock of the Bank of the United States, exclusive of the amount necessary to pay the interest on the bank loan, would be sufficient for the sinking fund to pay the installments on the bank loan, and sufficient, after 1802, to redeem yearly the deferred 6 per cent stock; (3) the interest on the stock redeemed by the foregoing appropriations; (4) the surplus of all revenues remaining at the end of the calendar year beyond appropriations charged on them; and (5) the proceeds of the sales of western lands.[33] These appropriations to the sinking fund were permanent and were to be inviolably pledged for the redemption or purchase of debt until the entire national debt had been discharged.[34]

Did Hamilton's Sinking Fund of 1795 Avoid the Error of Pitt's Sinking Fund? — The sinking fund which Hamilton proposed in 1795[35] has been described as "the most rigid that could be devised."[36] It has also been said that the "evil" of Pitt's sinking fund was incorporated by Hamilton into the American financial system.[37] The point emphasized by the critics of Hamilton was that the principle of an inviolable operation of a sinking fund was a main feature of Hamilton's plan of 1795. The danger in such a principle, it has also been asserted, was magnified by the new permanent sources of income appropriated to the sinking fund. Thus, the outbreak of a major war would have produced in the United States the same absurd results that occurred in England,

33. *Ibid.*, I, 327-28.
34. Madison, in a letter to Jefferson, expressed his dissatisfaction with Hamilton's plan, especially to its excessively long period of debt payment, in the following words: "Hamilton has, in an arrogant Valedictory Report, presented a plan for the purpose. It will require 30 *years* of uninterrupted operation. The fund is to consist of the surpluses of the import and excise, and the temporary duties of the last session. . . . You will judge of the chance of our ever being out of debt, if no other means are to be used" (Madison to Jefferson, February 15, 1795, *Letters and Other Writings of James Madison* [New York: R. Worthington, 1884], II, 36).
35. Hamilton's plan was accepted by Congress almost without change. See the act of March 3, 1795, entitled "An Act making further provision for the support of Public Credit, and for the redemption of the Public Debt" (*Statutes at Large*, I, 433-38).
36. Ross, p. 50.
37. Henry C. Adams, p. 265.

since Hamilton's sinking fund would have remained in full operation throughout the deficit period caused by war.

It would seem, however, that Hamilton was thoroughly aware of the danger in maintaining a sinking fund during a deficit period. He had no false conceptions of the possibility of extinguishing debt without creating a surplus of revenues over expenditures.[38] But Hamilton realized that "opinion is the soul" of public credit, and that without the inviolable application of a sinking fund the public creditors would conclude that they had no guarantee that the administration of government would exercise their public trust in the manner expected of them. It was necessary, therefore, to place the revenues needed to extinguish a national debt out of the hands of government.[39]

Hamilton was unlike the English financiers in that he anticipated the possibility that an inviolable sinking fund might be found operating in a deficit period. He took several measures to prevent the possibility that such an embarrassing situation would result, or, if the situation were unavoidable, to mitigate the results.

One precaution taken by Hamilton was that of trying to insure that an adequate margin existed between the total expenditures of government and the total cost of debt service. He estimated the total expenditures of $5,681,844 on the assumption of mild war conditions. The revenue estimate was $6,552,301. The total cost of debt service, including the interest on the public debt and the permanent income of the augmented sinking fund, would be $4,373,836. With regard to the difference between the latter figure and the total revenue, Hamilton remarked: "An expectation may be indulged that even foreign war . . . would not occasion a defalcation in the revenues greater than the difference." Associated with this precaution taken by Hamilton was his assumption that the productivity of the existing revenue system of the nation would increase considerably in the near future. The relationship between the demands of debt service and the revenues, Hamilton concluded, permitted the nation to adopt the inviolable principle "fearless of future embarrassment."[40]

Unlike Pitt's sinking fund, Hamilton's plan did not call for an ap-

38. Earlier in his report, Hamilton stated: "To extinguish a debt which exists, and to avoid the contracting more, are ideas always favored by public feeling and opinion; but to pay taxes for the one or the other purpose, which are the only means of avoiding the evil, is always, more or less, unpopular" (*American State Papers, Finance*, I, 331).

39. *Ibid.*, I, 332.   40. *Ibid.*

propriation to the sinking fund of a specific absolute amount. The only invariable requirement was that so much of the revenues had to be appropriated as would permit the redemption of the 6 per cent and 6 per cent deferred stocks according to the right of redemption reserved by the government. By this provision, the plan required that a minimum of $452,891 be permanently appropriated to the sinking fund, with the actual appropriation in any one year depending on the size of the surplus of revenue beyond appropriations. According to Hamilton, he purposely designed the sinking fund in this manner in order not to be faced with the situation of simultaneously devoting large sums to debt redemption and borrowing in order to finance a war. He stated that an absolute appropriation of a larger sum would not be prudent.[41]

Hamilton's proposed sinking fund of 1795 was basically different from all previously constituted sinking funds in that it provided for the partial suspension of the operation of a sinking fund during war. It was a sinking fund that was capable of adapting to different budgetary conditions: that is, instead of being the most rigid sinking fund that could be devised, it was a sinking fund possessing a significant degree of flexibility. Hamilton's provision for decreasing the rate of debt extinguishment during war was stated as follows:

> Provided, always, that, whenever THE FUND shall be more than sufficient for paying off . . . [the national debt] . . . within the term of thirty years, it shall be lawful for Congress, if at war with any foreign European Power, to apply so much of the excess as they may think fit . . . towards the expenses of such war.[42]

During a period of peace, therefore, surpluses of the revenues, which were required by Hamilton's plan to be appropriated to the sinking fund, would tend to place the rate of debt extinguishment ahead of that which was absolutely required by Hamilton's redemption schedule of thirty years. At the outbreak of a war with an European nation, the

41. *Ibid.*
42. *Ibid.*, I, 328. This feature of Hamilton's plan has never been previously pointed out. That it has gone unnoticed all these years is partly accounted for by the fact that it was not placed in the sinking fund legislation of 1795. Perhaps the most important reason for its being unnoticed is the complex organization of Hamilton's report, combined with an error on the part of Hamilton. Hamilton listed all of his "propositions" in one section of his report and his "remarks" on his propositions in another section. In his remarks on the provision in question, he referred to it as the last clause of the fifth proposition (*Ibid.*, I, 332). Actually, it was the last provision in the ninth clause of the fifth proposition.

part of the sinking fund's income which was not necessary to insure the ultimate redemption of the debt in 1826 could then be diverted to financing the war:

> This, while it secures the extinction of the existing debt within a reasonable term, by preventing too great a proportion of the public revenue from being tied up by the sinking fund, gives due weight to the consideration of providing for future emergencies.[43]

After having pointed out the various safeguards contained in his sinking fund plan, Hamilton concluded by saying, "There is no cause to hesitate about the inviolable appropriation of funds to the extinction of an existing debt within no less a term than thirty years."

43. *Ibid.*

7. BEYOND THE ORIGINS CONTROVERSY TO A NEW PERSPECTIVE ON HAMILTON'S FISCAL POLICIES

> *He touched the dead corpse of public credit, and it sprang upon its feet.*
> —DANIEL WEBSTER

Hamilton's role in establishing the nation's fiscal policies came to a close in 1795. The fate of the funding system, the sinking fund, and the national bank in the hands of succeeding Federalist and anti-Federalist administrations is another story. What is of interest here is whether the nation's fiscal foundation was, as Dunbar expressed it, "too much influenced by English precedent." But perhaps the origins controversy has been a misleading controversy in that the dogmatic question of "imitation" *vs.* "original invention" disguises the real significance of Hamilton's fiscal policies. An examination of the proofs of the nineteenth-century economists suggests that their search of Hamilton's fiscal edifice for evidence of copying from the English produced a mass of evidence for their position, but also an analysis which was rather dated and sterile. After the following summary of these proofs, the conclusions of the present study will be made.

PROOFS OF THE ENGLISH IMITATION THESIS

In attributing English origins to Hamilton's fiscal policies, the economists used a rather simple procedure. Hamilton's main fiscal edifices — the bank, the funding system, and the sinking fund — could all be said to have their counterparts or models in eighteenth-century England. If an impressive number of parallels or similarities could be shown to exist between Hamilton's policies and the English models, then it could be concluded that since the English fiscal policies existed first, Hamilton's fiscal policies must have been blind imitations of the English models.

73

The Sinking Fund. — The most important of Hamilton's fiscal policies from the standpoint of the origins controversy is the sinking fund, because the strongest statements of the English imitation thesis have been made regarding that policy. Even Dunbar, who approached the subject in a more sympathetic manner than the other nineteenth-century economists, stated that Hamilton's sinking fund was "unmistakably adopted from English legislation." The sinking fund was "the last new thing in finance and full of promise." "Without doubt," Dunbar continued, "Hamilton in this matter followed Mr. Pitt."[1]

The administration of the sinking funds was strikingly similar in both countries. Hamilton proposed the establishment of a "Board of Commissioners, composed (like Pitt's) of high officers of state, in whom should be invested the control of a fund, to be applied to the purchase or payment of debt, and continue so invested until the whole of the debt should be discharged."[2]

More important to the argument of the economists was the question of the sinking fund's method of operation. It was pointed out that sinking fund legislation in the United States copied the English precedent by not regarding stock (government securities) purchased by the sinking fund commissioners as being retired and, instead, letting such purchased stock continue to bear interest, which, in turn, was used to made additional purchases. The operation of Hamilton's sinking fund was modeled exactly after Pitt's, according to Dunbar, because "they both in fact depended for their efficiency upon the same essential principle, — the compounding of interest by the investment of interest accruing on purchases already made."[3] To make the replica exact, Hamilton's sinking fund was "appropriated and pledged firmly and inviolably" to the purchase of debt, whatever the condition of the Treasury otherwise.

The proponents of the English imitation thesis were also emphatic on the point that Hamilton held to the same basic theory of a sinking fund as the English sinking fund theorists. The principle of inviolable payments was the logical outgrowth, according to the economists, of the idea that a sinking fund could perform magic in paying off debt within a short period of time. Any temporary cessation of its operation would prevent the fund from acquiring the full benefits of a sum growing at compound interest. Adams believed that in all these respects Hamilton's

1. Dunbar, pp. 82, 85.   2. *Ibid.*, p. 85.   3. *Ibid.*, p. 86.

ideas conformed to those of Dr. Price.[4] Pitt's sinking fund of 1786 was in administration, operation, and theory based upon the teachings of Dr. Price. Thus, the economists thought, Hamilton, in copying Pitt's fiscal policies, accepted the erroneous principles of Price.

Ross stressed the point that Hamilton's sinking fund was the most "rigid" and inflexible type of sinking fund that could be devised.[5] Hamilton would have continued the operation of the sinking fund through periods of budgetary deficits such as would occur during war, during which periods borrowed money would be the sinking fund's source of income. Ross admitted, however, that no circumstances occurred during Hamilton's administration to test this point.

The Funding System. — The principal argument which has been advanced to show English principles in Hamilton's funding system is that funding systems in both countries were based on the idea of perpetuity financing. Adams remarked that Hamilton either believed in a perpetual debt or was ignorant of the consequences of his policies.[6] Dunbar's case for showing Hamilton's use of English precedents in his funding system was based on the similarities between English debt instruments and the debt instruments proposed by Hamilton.[7]

Particular attention was paid by Dunbar to Hamilton's abortive proposal to introduce a tontine loan into American finance. This "ill-advised" scheme was, according to Dunbar's puritanical orientation, the "least credible of Hamilton's propositions." To Dunbar, the tontine proposal was rather conclusive evidence of Hamilton's disposition to follow English precedents in finance. He commented that the details in Hamilton's tontine were "adjusted upon the plan of the English tontine of 1789, which had been brought out by Mr. Pitt a few months before the date of Hamilton's report."[8]

The National Bank. — Hamilton's Bank of the United States has been declared a copy of the Bank of England by numerous writers. All commentators take the same general approach as did Dunbar. As evidence that the Bank of England was the model, Dunbar relied heavily on a comparison of the charters of the American and English banks. He placed the acts establishing the two banks side by side and compared the sections enumerating their powers:

4. Henry C. Adams, pp. 262-65.
5. Ross, p. 50.
6. Henry C. Adams, pp. 161-62.
7. Dunbar, p. 77.
8. *Ibid.*, p. 78.

[Act of February 25, 1791]

The said corporation may sell any part of the public debt whereof its stock shall be composed, but shall not be at liberty to purchase any public debt whatsoever; nor shall directly or indirectly deal or trade in anything, except bills of exchange, gold or silver bullion, or in the sale of goods really and truly pledged for money lent and not redeemed in due time; or of goods which shall be the produce of its lands. Neither shall the said corporation take more than at the rate of six per centum per annum, for or upon its loans or discounts.

[Act of 5 Will. and Mary, c. 20.] xxvii. [That the corporation shall not deal in Goods, Wares, or Merchandise.] xxviii. Provided, That nothing herein contained shall in any ways be construed to hinder the said Corporation from dealing in Bills of Exchange, or in buying or selling Bullion, Gold, or Silver, or in selling any Goods, Wares or Merchandise whatsoever, which shall really and *bona fide* be left or deposited with the said Corporation for Money lent and advanced thereon, and which shall not be redeemed at the Time agreed on, or within three Months after, or from selling such Goods as shall or may be the produce of Lands purchased by the said Corporation.[9]

The similarities between many of the provisions in the two acts were considered by Dunbar and others as more than accidental. It has been remarked that Hamilton copied the Bank of England by making the bank subscriptions payable in public debt. Several other striking similarities have also been pointed out. Otenasek has said, "It is obvious that the first Bank of the United States was modeled almost exclusively on the Bank of England."[10]

A New Interpretation of Hamilton's Fiscal Policies

Prior to the acceptance of the Jeffersonian English imitation thesis by the nineteenth-century economists, the only alternative explanation for the origins of Hamilton's fiscal policies had been the opinion, advanced mainly by the Hamiltonian Federalists, that Hamilton's fiscal policies were original inventions. But this interpretation is also untenable in its naive form, for the similarities between English and Hamiltonian fiscal policies are too striking to be accidental. Hamilton's policies obviously did not evolve entirely independently of the English experience.

A middle-ground position, conceivably, could be advanced which

9. *Ibid.*, p. 92.

10. Otenasek, pp. 65-66.

would portray Hamilton as variously copying and originating the several components of his fiscal program. But, although this approach can be shown to conform with the facts to a greater degree than the antithetical positions of originator and copyist, this middle-ground position fails to provide a vehicle for emphasizing the essentials of Hamiltonian finance and their relevance for twentieth-century fiscal policy.

Symbols of Orthodoxy. — Only in appearances were Hamilton's fiscal policies copies of the English fiscal policies. Their outward appearances were English — but their purposes and operation were quite different from their English counterparts and conformed to the demands created by the vastly different American situation. Nor did Hamilton share English fiscal theory. Hamilton's involvement in copying the English models was confined mainly to such superficial matters as forms, name, and administrative organization of fiscal policies.

The main point is that Hamilton's contribution to American fiscal policy was not in his being either a copyist or an original inventor, although in some respects he was both, but in his knowing how to disguise politically unacceptable policies in the wrappings of orthodoxy to achieve essential ends within a minimum of time. His objective was the establishment of public credit. To achieve this objective, Hamilton employed methods which involved him in what is perhaps the greatest pretense in American fiscal policy history. He felt that the quick achievement of this important goal was worth the risk of exposure and condemnation by Jefferson. The alternative would have been to try to establish public credit by taking the nation through a long period of austerity in order to prove the public credit by painfully paying off the national debt. Gradually, perhaps, the new nation would have had its credit established at home and in the great financial centers of Europe. But in the interim the nation might have become weak, divided, or subjected to foreign domination.[11] Hamilton was not willing to wait for the establishment of credit nor to go through this period of national sacrifice. He felt that national credit was an urgent matter.

Hamilton's sense of strategy was not influenced by the financial precepts in *Poor Richard's Almanac.* Instead, his strategy was based on his conviction that mankind was led more by "sounds and appearances"

11. This alternative method of attempting to establish public credit probably would have been the method pursued by Jefferson. See John Spencer Basset, *The Federalist System 1789-1801,* Vol. II of *The American Nation: A History,* ed. A. B. Hart (28 vols.; New York: Harper & Bros., 1906), p. 29.

than by rational demonstrations. The orthodox symbols of sound finance were what influenced mankind in its estimates of the degree of the establishment of public credit. For instance, in spite of England's adherence to erroneous ideas in public finance, the public credit of England was high. The symbols of orthodoxy in public finance were precisely those policies which flourished in England and which are at issue in the origins controversy — the bank, the sinking fund, and the funding system. Transplanted to America, altered for the different conditions, stripped of their erroneous doctrines, and redirected to serve different purposes — but all the while retaining their outward appearances — these symbols of orthodoxy were then incorporated by Hamilton into his plan for the establishment of public credit.

When Hamilton took office, the American public was full of anxiety about his approach to what they regarded an urgent problem — the payment of the national debt. In the mind of the public, the symbol of orthodoxy to handle this problem was a sinking fund. Speculators in government securities, like William Bingham, pleaded for the establishment of fiscal policies based upon the English models. Even Jefferson had been impressed by the calculations of Dr. Price. In fact, throughout his administration Hamilton was under constant pressure from the public, Congress, and President Washington to make a "secure provision" for the extinguishment of the national debt. Hamilton obliged: he gave the American public a sinking fund.

It is true that Hamilton believed in the magic of a sinking fund, but not in its ability magically to pay off debt. The magic that the sinking fund and other English fiscal policies would perform was in their ability to alter mankind's appraisal of a new country's public credit. Hamilton gambled on the strategy that the use of symbols of orthodoxy in fiscal policy would produce the appearance of financial maturity and stability — and the pretense worked. Opinions in the United States and abroad quickly changed. Within a year, the United States was borrowing in Europe on terms as favorable as England and the other financial powers of Europe enjoyed.

Hamilton's basic assumption, that mankind is led more by sounds and appearances than by realities, led him to the conclusion that the public could be led by a "useful illusion." This outlook can be found in Hamilton's private correspondence on financial subjects at an early date. In 1779, Hamilton presented the argument that the Continental bills of credit had ended in depreciation because of a lack of confidence in the emissions, and not because of an excessive quantity in circulation. To remedy the situation, he proposed the issuance of a new paper circulation based on a plan similar to the one John Law had carried out in France. This plan, by uniting the government with the moneyed interests and other private individuals, would produce the needed illusion to secure the public's confidence in a new paper circulation. The proposal also called for changing the monetary unit from the dollar to the pound. He believed the pound would generate greater confidence because "Mankind are much led by sounds and appearances." At a later date, Hamilton suggested that "good landed security" might provide the illusion necessary to give a paper circulation the needed confidence.

When Hamilton took public office, he could not, of course, be so explicit about the use of illusory methods. But there is still sufficient internal evidence in Hamilton's public reports to show that his basic outlook on human nature had not changed since his early correspondence on financial subjects. In his first Report on Public Credit, Hamilton emphasized the importance of "appearances" in the establishment of public credit, and again made a distinction between the influence of "appearances as well as realities" on the opinions of mankind. After the symbols of orthodoxy had been incorporated into American public finance, Hamilton never ceased in attempting to give his policies as much publicity as possible. If the sinking fund made some purchases of debt, Hamilton would send circulars to the newspapers; if America obtained a loan at a favorable rate in the foreign markets, Hamilton would have this announced in the financial centers of the United States.

Hamilton, not Jefferson, was the financier. The difference in the two men was that Hamilton was able to discern the truly essential goal to be pursued in fiscal policy. The goal to which Hamilton gave priority was the establishment of public credit, not the paying off of the national debt. Jefferson, on the other hand, made a fetish out of debt extinguishment at a time when such a goal was impossible to reach. Hamilton's greatness was in his capacity to give priority to the important goals, and to win delay in obtaining conflicting subsidiary goals until they could be properly handled. Thus in 1795 Hamilton believed that the public revenues had developed sufficiently to begin earnest debt reduction. In his report of 1795, he finally advanced debt extinguishment to a place of major importance, since the public credit had already been established.

Hamilton's ability to time properly the goals of fiscal policy has not been recognized. Instead, it has been said that he showed inconsistency in advocating at one time the principle that "a national debt is a

79

national blessing," and at another time that the national debt must be placed in the process of extinguishment. One writer concluded that it was not possible to reconcile all of Hamilton's remarks.[12] But the apparent inconsistencies of Hamilton's statements vanish if the context is examined, and if one keeps in mind Hamilton's priorities in timing fiscal policies. When Hamilton first made his classic remark that "a national debt, if it is not excessive, will be to us a national blessing," he was not discussing the perpetuation of debt, but the feasibility of paying off the debt. Specifically, the year was 1780, and he was trying to calculate how long it would take to pay off the Revolutionary debt after the peace. Some pessimists had feared that the debt had grown so large that it would be beyond the country's ability ever to pay it. Hamilton confidently replied that the debt could be paid off within twenty years, if necessary: "Any doubt," he added, "must originate from gross ignorance." The famous quotation followed — not with the intent of advocating a perpetual debt, but with the intent of pointing out that while the debt was in the process of extinguishment, it would serve a useful purpose, that is, the united effort to pay off the debt over an extended period of time would help cement the union of the separate states.

From what has been said, it does not follow that Hamilton's fiscal policies had their value only in a psychological sense and were without a substantive basis of operation. Hamilton realized that the building of confidence, although depending chiefly upon "sounds and appearances," also depended upon other factors. Hamilton's conversion plan, which reduced the annual cost of debt service in the early years of the new nation, was vital to the success of those policies that relied on "sounds and appearances" for their effectiveness. Given the new nation's immature revenue system, it would have been impossible to meet the interest burden on the debt in its original form. If a time ever existed in the United States when a balanced budget, in the sense of revenues sufficient to cover expenditures (including payments for interest on the national debt), was imperative, it was at the beginning of Hamilton's administration. Perhaps the almost unbounded faith in the inherent virtues of a balanced budget which developed in the United States in later years can be partly traced to this special case where, in fact, a balanced budget was the *sine qua non* of putting the nation's finances in order. There is no question that the Bank of the United States, in performing its fiscal

12. Charles J. Bullock, *Selected Readings in Public Finance* (2d ed.; Boston: Ginn and Company, 1920), p. 828.

agency services, made an important contribution to the business and commercial community and to the smooth operation of the Treasury. Also, the sinking fund performed a real financial service in its purchases of debt below par. And, the funding system, by assuming the regular payment of interest to bondholders, had a substantive basis as solid as any policy could have. To the individual bondholder, it made no difference whether public credit had been established by sounds and appearances or by other means; what did matter was the real phenomenon that public debt was selling above par.

In summing up the nature of the Hamiltonian system of finance, it should be pointed out that there was, after all, a rather strong basis for the support of an English imitation thesis, for there were obvious similarities between the English and Hamiltonian systems. But this is precisely the appearance Hamilton wanted to create. What the nineteenth-century economists did not see was that under these superficial wrappings of orthodoxy was an entirely different system of finance — one based upon a certain assumption concerning human nature, and upon different purposes and theoretical moorings. In transplanting these policies to the American environment, Hamilton did more than modify them: he changed their basic meaning. Dunbar's intuition was correct, although he couldn't explain it — Hamilton was a great financial statesman. The Hamiltonian policies were highly appropriate for the fiscal problems of the day. In attacking the Hamiltonian fiscal edifice, the nineteenth-century economists were forced, by the absence of any clearly erroneous principles, to attack it by tracing its origin to the obviously fallacious English model. The image of Hamilton as a great financial statesman is thus reconciled with the existence of parallels between his policies and those of the English. The question of whether his use of illusory methods qualifies him as a "Machiavellian" statesman is a question that can probably be answered in the affirmative. Popular suspicion has been vindicated.

Present-Day Fiscal Policy. — The origins controversy has focused attention on those aspects of Hamiltonian finance that were similar to English finance. When the English fiscal policies were exposed for what they led to — a financial fiasco as great or greater than the South Sea Bubble — then Hamilton's fiscal policies were relegated to antiquarian interest. Little, if anything, remained in his policies to serve as models for modern fiscal policy. The new interpretation of Hamilton's financial system offered here indicates that Hamilton's policies and assumptions are indeed relevant to present-day fiscal policies.

81

The Hamiltonian precedent was a fiscal system characterized by (1) a priority of goals based upon an understanding of the dangers, conditions, and institutions of the time, (2) flexibility and timing to conform with changing conditions and goals, and (3) the use of symbols of orthodoxy, properly modified, to serve as a means to gain acceptance of otherwise politically unacceptable policies. Fiscal policy practices and theory since 1929 can produce several examples of policies and proposals which, in the sense that they contained all or most of the above characteristics, were significantly Hamiltonian in their nature.

During the last year of the Hoover administration, a historically unimportant but interesting proposal was made by the Under Secretary of the Treasury, Ogden L. Mills. Though the administration's attempts to balance the budget had been ineffective, President Hoover was still of the opinion that a balanced budget was the keystone of economic recovery.[13] The administration, because it continued to include statutory debt retirements in the expenditure totals in computing a surplus or a deficit, at times tried to give the impression that the situation was not as serious as commonly imagined.[14] Stating this idea somewhat more forcefully, Secretary Mills, recalling the accelerated debt reduction of the 1920's, argued that the excess of debt retirement of the preceding decade over the statutory requirements had, in effect, created a reserve. In lean years, therefore, debt retirement could be postponed in relation to the size of the reserve accumulated. This proposal was strikingly similar to Hamilton's provision for temporarily suspending the operation of a sinking fund in the event of war with a foreign power. A faithful application of the Hamiltonian precedent would have publicly demonstrated that, because of the reserve, the long-run objective of debt repayment was still being honored, and that the special circumstances of major depression permitted a temporary suspension of debt retirement and a balanced budget. The politically unacceptable could have been made palatable, and could have saved the Hoover administration from much of its embarrassment.

There is a very suggestive parallel between the early days of the Roosevelt administration and the Hamiltonian precedent. Just as the symbols of sound finance in 1790 were the English fiscal policies, the ultimate in fiscal orthodoxy in 1933 was the annually balanced budget. But the Hoover administration, beset by rising expenditures and de-

13. Kimmel, p. 148.

14. *Ibid.*, p. 151.

clining revenues, had failed to achieve orthodoxy's goal. In his campaign, Roosevelt took the politically logical position of denouncing the unorthodox financing of the Hoover administration, and promising the electorate that a Democratic victory would mean a reduction in expenditures and a balanced budget.[15] The parallel present in the early New Deal period is that, like Hamilton, Roosevelt gave the appearance of conforming to orthodoxy, but did not strictly live up to orthodox standards in practice. Hamilton's initial program did not set up a sinking fund to start seriously paying off debt; nor did Roosevelt's campaigning on a platform of orthodoxy bring about a balanced budget. Just as Hamilton used the sinking fund, to paraphrase Jefferson, as a machine to give the impression of debt repayment, so Roosevelt established a sort of dual budget whereby the budget, counting just "general" expenditures, appeared to be in balance, but because of "emergency" expenditures was actually running a deficit. At this point the parallel fails, as Hamilton was successful in achieving his objective, the establishment of public credit, but Roosevelt failed in his objective of restoring the depressed American economy.[16]

COMPARISON OF ENGLISH AND HAMILTONIAN FISCAL POLICIES

The English sinking fund had only one purpose for its existence: the rapid extinguishment of the national debt. This policy grew out of England's early experience with a national debt during a period in which the concept of a surplus budget had not come into being. A scheme was needed to wipe out the debt. What the proponents of the sinking fund claimed they had found was comparable to what the alchemists had hoped to find, that is, some universal and magical solvent for public debts. The belief in the efficacy of a sinking fund beguiled the whole English nation for about a century.

Hamilton's sinking fund had many purposes, the principal one being the appearance it created of having a nation's financial house in order. Jefferson's suspicions were not too far from the truth. Hamilton was using the sinking fund as a "puzzle," not to confound the legislature, as Jefferson argued, but to confound the public in general, and the financial and propertied classes in particular. The debt ostensibly was on its way to extinction, but Hamilton knew that the immature state

15. *Ibid.*, pp. 165-66.
16. However, Roosevelt might be classified as successful, if his "strategic" goal is viewed as being primarily political; that is, prevention of a radical solution to the Great Depression and the preservation of constitutional government.

of the nation's revenue system did not permit the introduction in 1790 of a serious plan to extinguish the national debt. Hence, Hamilton feigned debt reduction. He also had the ability to convert this symbol of orthodoxy to other purposes, including a purpose comparable to the open market operations of central banks today. When the time came that debt repayment was possible, Hamilton was willing to make the sinking fund's purpose that of debt repayment, if appropriate modifications and safeguards in its operation were made. Hamilton's claim of orthodoxy to other purposes, including a purpose comparable to the but in his ability to take this fiscal policy and convert it to useful and valid purposes.

Of extreme importance in revealing the weaknesses of the English imitation thesis is the question of whether Hamilton's sinking fund was the most "rigid" type of sinking fund possible. The argument of this study is that Hamilton's sinking fund, in its early stages, was so small in resources that the question is irrelevant. More important is the discovery that Hamilton's proposed sinking fund of 1795, which was to acquire a sizable income, contained an escape clause which made it a flexible sinking fund. Its operation would have been analogous to present-day counter-cyclical fiscal policy. In the sinking fund's case, the problem was war instead of the business cycle. The sinking fund would get ahead of its scheduled debt redemption during peacetime, and during wartime its operation would be partially suspended. The extent of the sinking fund purchases during deficit periods would not be of any great importance, and the possibility for any absurd results would be minimized by certain other safeguards. These provisions completely refute the contention that Hamilton's sinking fund of 1795 was modeled after the rigid type of sinking fund of Pitt's administration. Hamilton foresaw the difficulties inherent in an inviolable sinking fund, which the English did not see, and he proposed the needed flexibility.

Purpose of Hamilton's Funding System. — The English funding system was a means of raising revenue, an alternative to taxation in financing increased government expenditures. Its special advantage over other systems of borrowing was that the government had to provide only for the interest on the debt and not for the principal. The funding system in England worked through the privileged companies, such as the South Sea Company, the East India Company, and the Bank of England. It operated by the incorporation of debt in these privileged companies, which, because they wanted continued corporate life, were willing to give up the claims on the principal of the debt in return for interest payments and special monopoly rights. The concept of a perpetual debt was definitely an outgrowth of this type of a funding system.

Hamilton's funding system, in contrast, was never used for raising revenue to finance a current deficit. The different problems existing in the United States led to a new application of the funding principle. The funding system was used by Hamilton as a policy for a debt already in existence, rather than for the creation of debt. Hamilton's administration had deficits, but they were financed by temporary loans that called for the early payment of both interest and principal. The American funding system, moreover, had no parallel to the English practice of funding a debt by the creation of privileged companies. Perpetuity financing was not inherent to the funding system proposed and administered by Hamilton.

Hamilton's funding system was part of his plan to adopt policies that produced sounds and appearances which would work toward the early establishment of public credit. The handling of the Revolutionary debt prior to 1789 had been a national disgrace. The weak pre-Constitutional government could not even meet the interest on the debt, much less the principal. Arrearages of interest were mounting annually. Hamilton wanted to dissociate the national debt of the new government from the debt of the old government, and still keep faith with the public creditors. He struck boldly to accomplish this by his policies of conversion and funding: the conversion policy would call in all the old securities in exchange for new issues, and the funding system would pledge enough revenues to the creditors to assure them that the interest on the new issues would be faithfully met. Hamilton's move to establish a funding system had such an impact on the public's judgment of the future public credit of the United States that Hamilton was able to obtain a reduction in the average rate of interest on the debt in the conversion operation. This was an unprecedented accomplishment, because a nation's ability to convert a debt to a lower rate of interest usually follows, not precedes, the establishment of public credit. Hamilton relied on the public's confidence in funding systems to achieve this remarkable result. Other than in name, what Hamilton's funding system had in common with the English model was that in both cases the government was obligated to pay only the interest on the debt.[17] The new nation could meet this obligation but not the obligation of paying the principal.

17. This interpretation of the purpose of Hamilton's sinking fund depends on an understanding of what "funding" meant in the eighteenth century — not

A National Bank for Economic Development. — The Bank of England eventually became a mainstay in the British economy, and a central bank. During most of the eighteenth century, however, the Bank of England was part of the English funding system, and primarily a vehicle for permanent government loans. It had originated as a scheme for financing a deficit and was repeatedly exploited by the government for additional loans. Originally, the bank was not oriented towards the needs of the private economy. It was a tool of state, and remained primarily so during the period in which Hamilton allegedly copied it.

On the other hand, the Bank of the United States was never a part of the American funding system. No permanent loans were furnished to the American government by Hamilton's national bank. Temporary loans were granted the government by the bank, but the government also borrowed on a temporary basis from other banks. More important is the consideration that Hamilton's national bank had as its main economic purpose that of aiding the development of the private economy. Hamilton could see the bank performing that function partly through its ability to pool money capital for lending purposes, and partly through its ability to raise confidence in the business community, but mainly by its ability to provide a satisfactory medium of exchange. Perhaps Hamilton exaggerated the "lack" of money in the economy; nevertheless, his main purpose was clear. Through an agency capable of acquiring the public's confidence, such as a national bank under private control, an auxiliary medium would be provided to aid in the economic development needed by a nation which was young and still politically unstable.

The Bank of the United States also fitted perfectly into Hamilton's strategy of using symbols of orthodoxy for establishing public credit. There was no particular reason why Hamilton could not have obtained the desired economic results mentioned above by promoting a system of state banks. The fact of the matter is that Hamilton's national bank had no monopoly privileges, and state banks, including the Bank of

---

what "funding" or "refunding" means today. No policy of Hamilton's has been subject to such varied misconceptions as his plan to fund the debt. The existing studies on the subject indicate that the writers either have lost sight of the meaning of "funding," or are discussing one of Hamilton's other policies, such as the conversion policy. Hamilton's own words explain precisely what he meant by a funding system. To him, to fund a debt meant "to *pledge* specified and adequate funds for the regular payment of interest till the principal . . . [is] reimbursed." *Works of . . . Hamilton,* VIII, 436.

New York which Hamilton helped found, flourished alongside it. But a national bank gave the appearance of a mature financial system. Hamilton's cleverness manifested itself by again using a symbol of orthodoxy, not only for the psychological purpose mentioned, but for a tangible purpose — raising the price of government securities. He thus made the bank's stock payable partly in government securities, creating a demand for government securities which would help reinforce the funding system and the sinking fund in establishing national credit.

A Financial System for a Political Purpose. — The above sketch of the contrasts between Hamilton's fiscal policies and their English counterparts can be summarized by referring again to the special national environments in which the two sets of fiscal policies arose and flourished. It was the argument of Chapters 2 and 3 that English fiscal policies developed gradually and piecemeal, without much forethought, during a century when the English government was plagued by foreign wars and was poorly stocked with knowledge concerning public finance. But Hamilton's ostensibly similar fiscal policies were tailored for establishing the public credit of a new nation composed of a union of separate states plagued by the possibilities of disunion or a rebirth of foreign domination. In a real sense, the English policies were designed to delay or to put off forever the solving of a problem — the problem of raising taxation to a level sufficient to meet the ever-growing expenditure demands of a nation entangled in the political alignments of eighteenth-century Europe. But Hamilton's policies constituted a cleverly designed fiscal program to bring quickly about the fiscal maturity and stability of a newly created national state.

The Hamiltonian biographers are correct in portraying Hamilton as a nation builder. Hamilton's critics, in emphasizing Hamilton's lack of financial experience commensurate with the job of Secretary of the Treasury, have missed the real meaning of Hamilton's administration. Specifically, Hamilton was not particularly concerned about financial subjects in the sense exhibited by the English financiers. He was, in contrast, concerned with the impact of financial and economic institutions upon the nation's growth and unity. The English fiscal policies, in short, were relatively crude financial expedients whose purposes were almost strictly financial; but Hamilton's policies had purposes that can be classified as almost wholly political, including fostering an economic environment that would support the political ends. More so than Montagu, Walpole, or Pitt, he was the great financier of the times.

87

UNIVERSITY OF FLORIDA MONOGRAPHS

Social Sciences